In 2022, Geoff Hutchison hung up his headphones after a long career as an ABC broadcaster. Before that, he was a journalist on the *7.30 Report* and a one-time *Foreign Correspondent*. Geoff is intensely curious and has seldom worked a day in his life. It has been one of great privilege: talking to people, witnessing extraordinary moments and coming to the understanding that the things we share are far more significant than those that divide us.

HOW NOT TO BECOME A GRUMPY OLD BUGGER

GEOFF HUTCHISON

 affirm press

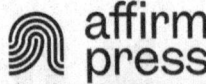

First published in Australia in 2025 by Affirm Press,
a Simon & Schuster (Australia) Pty Limited company
Bunurong/Boon Wurrung Country
28 Thistlethwaite Street, South Melbourne VIC 3205

Affirm Press is located on the unceded land of the Bunurong/Boon Wurrung peoples of the Kulin Nation. Affirm Press pays respect to their Elders past and present.

New York Amsterdam/Antwerp London Toronto Sydney/Melbourne New Delhi
Visit our website at www.simonandschuster.com.au

AFFIRM PRESS and design are trademarks of Affirm Press Pty Ltd, Inc.,
used under licence by Simon & Schuster, LLC.

10 9 8 7 6 5 4 3

© Geoff Hutchison 2025

All rights reserved. No part of this publication may be reproduced, stored in a retrieval system, or transmitted in any form or by any means, electronic, mechanical, photocopying, recording or otherwise, without prior permission of the publisher.

The moral rights of the author have been asserted.

 A catalogue record for this book is available from the National Library of Australia

9781923046757 (paperback)
9781761636806 (ebook)

Cover design by Dev Parry
Typeset in Garamond Premier Pro by J&M Typesetting
Printed and bound in Australia by the Opus Group

For Dad,
and Blokes everywhere.

Contents

Introduction	Who This Book Is For	1
1	Are Men in Crisis?	3
2	Does This Make You Grumpy?	11
2 and a Bit	Why I Love Being a Bloke	30
3	Thinking About Retirement	32
4	Money	55
5	Influencer Interlude	62
6	The Harm Online	68
7	Your Health	78
8	Take a Look in the Mirror	89
9	Why We Have to Work at Friendships	96
10	Talking Footy	110
11	Secret Sorrows	121
12	Your Sexual Health	129
12 and a Bit	Keeping the Calcium Score	138
13	No Excuse for Violence	140
14	Hearing and Listening	153
15	Learning What the Kids Are Learning Online	162
16	Difference	172
17	Crisis, What Crisis?	183
17 and a Bit	A Career-Ending Kiss	198
18	What Makes a Life Worth Living?	203

19	Regrets	210
20	Giving the Future a Try	222
21	Death	232
22	A Word from My Son	242
23	A Grumpy Relapse	253
24	A Visit to the Doctor	256
25	Finding Contentment	261
26	Imagine It	273
Conclusion	Needing to Hear Dad's Voice	277
Resources		279

Introduction

Who This Book Is For

When I was just a kid, I asked my dad a pretty innocent question. I wanted to know if he was happy. His answer formed part of my motivation for writing this book.

Dad, like many men before him and many since, wore the often-chafing, tight-fitting uniform of male expectation. Father. Provider. Decision-maker. He was brought up to behave in a certain way. Life's parameters were clearly defined.

But was he happy? I don't think so. As Dad drifted into his retirement years, he seemed fatigued and fed up and a bit lost. In a fast-changing world, he became remote and withdrawn.

And not much fun to be around.

Grumpy.

I don't want to fall into the same trap, and I don't want you to either.

The trap of finding fault in others.

Needing to correct and lecture, rather than listening without judgement.

And I reckon, whether we are a forty-something or a ninety-something, Australian men are vulnerable. Too many of us seem to be missing out on a better life, because over time we lose our patience and kindness and our ability to connect.

Less sure of our roles. Uncertain about our futures. And often lonely because of it.

In this book, I hope to reassure you and tease you and probably annoy you a bit. But I truly believe that if we are prepared to open up a little to our partners and kids, if we become better mates with our mates, and if we look after our health and wellbeing with diligence rather than indifference, then we have so much to look forward to.

I hope something in this book resonates with you. And if your partner chooses to read bits of it aloud in bed at night, don't get all grumpy and pull the covers over your head. They just might be onto something.

Chapter 1

Are Men in Crisis?

It is summer. February of 1976, I think. I'm not sure. I am twelve years old, so a couple of months shy of becoming a teenager. Tall, skinny, sunburnt and in my speedos.

And holding an axe.

It is bloody hot. We live in the Perth Hills, many miles from the coast. The Fremantle Doctor won't arrive for an hour, if it doesn't run out of puff before then. Any movement in the gums comes from the relentless easterly that has been blowing hot, gritty air off the desert for days now.

Next door, the Stovell boys are in the pool. It is one of those Clark above-ground ones – not quite the real thing, but fit for purpose and the best we've got around here. Truth is, it was great when it was new, but now the water is glossy and slick with the fur of old Sandy, Mr Stovell's fat labrador, who not only gets to swim in it, but has, to our great and curious disgust, begun to grow an enormous cancer on his balls.

So no swimming for me, thanks. I have chores to do and a forest to fell. I am a lumberjack and I'm okay.

Dad works for the postmaster-general. Jarrah telegraph poles, presumably surplus to the requirements of the nation's telecommunications network – or perhaps not – regularly fall off the back of a truck, ready to be chainsawed and further refined by me to heat our water.

The pink meat is beautiful and compliant, and the axe head is sharp and persuasive. I finish by splitting kindling, delighting in the precision of a blade that, in my skilled hands, cuts, slices and juliennes, just like those K-Tel ads on the telly.

I'm good at this. And I've just lopped off the plonk-sodden head of Sir John Kerr. Dad reckons he's 'a bastard' for betraying Gough the way he did, and a few months on, the rage is being maintained. Life's battlelines have always been clearly defined at 19 Headingly Road. Apparently, we don't much trust Liberals or Victorians or the monarchy. All of which sits pretty well with me. As manhood beckons, I reckon I've got a keen grasp of things. What I'm good at and whose side I am on.

I'm good at chopping wood, playing cricket and tennis, doing Frank Spencer impressions and making friends. I am not very good at maths or, now that I have just started high school, convincing Julie Duxbury to keep going around with me. She has her eye on Mark Sutton, who carries a swagger and quite possibly cigarettes about him, which will prove irresistible. I don't smoke or swear aloud or chuck rocks at cars. I have lovely manners and a slight lisp. Mark Sutton does not fear me.

But nor do such things trouble me for long. I have a breezy, hopeful and curious disposition.

And so – having collected a big armful of wood, now nestled between elbow and wrist – cheery, chirpy me looks up to see Dad in his work overalls, wandering down towards me.

We live on a deep, three-quarter-of-an-acre block in Kalamunda. Our neat solid-brick three-by-one sits high on the hill, and a gravel driveway slides down past the back lawn and the sheds to a chook yard and beyond that to Dad's fruit and veggie garden.

He's off to water his tomatoes or try to fix the bore or ponder why the apricots taste so floury this year.

And out of nowhere, motivated by nothing other than the arrival of the question in my head, I ask him, 'How are you, Dad?'

He pauses. Says nothing, so I follow up with something altogether more innocently profound.

'Are you happy, Dad?'

He gives me a faint smile. Looks past me for a moment and then replies. 'No, not really.'

And then, as if we've just updated each other on the cricket score, he walks away beyond my questions to tend his garden and to keep his secrets.

I have no memory of how I processed his words. I probably asked 'Are you happy, Dad?' because I was fully expecting the reassuring warmth of the affirmation: 'Yes, mate, I am.'

What I got was: 'No, not really.'

There was no elaboration. No hasty attempt to reset, or to spare my feelings should they be hurt. Not that they were. I had no context or understanding beyond seeking to take the temperature of the moment. Dad was just Dad.

Without giving it a second thought, I carried my load of wood up to the house, while the Stovell boys busied themselves trying to drown each other.

'Clark pools, better than a beach in your own backyard!'

~

What did I know about my dad? What do boys really know about their fathers? Not much. Not unless the father wants to share his personal history. And Dad seldom did.

I knew he was born the third of seven kids and his childhood was shadowed by the hunger and poverty of the Great Depression. He was bright but shy and escaped school at thirteen to deliver bread alongside Ted Watson on the baker's cart. He loved Ted – my words, not his. It was Ted who first taught him how to roll a cigarette. It was Ted who bought him his first pair of long pants. It was Ted who …

A pivotal figure in Dad's life, Ted drowned while prawning in the Swan River one hot January night in 1939. He must have lost his footing in the muddy riverbed. His body was never found. And just like that, Dad lost the most important figure of his young life. Hours later, he sat atop the cart, delivering bread on his own.

I had to wait until Dad was eighty-two before he quietly revealed that story as we both stood under a brilliant night sky on the long-abandoned railway line that used to run from Midland to the hills. He was always happiest there, with a bit of bush around him and with the old laterite-stone house of his childhood just over yonder.

'Mum and Dad were a bit worried about me for a while,' he whispered. And he said no more.

While others enlisted in 1939 to fight in faraway battlefields, Dad was legally 'manpowered' out of uniform by his employer to stay home and continue to work as an apprentice baker. An essential industry required his skills. People needed bread every day.

Those inverted commas. 'Manpowered.'

I've often pondered this. Guiltily. Two of my uncles joined up and my Aunty Avis enrolled in the Australian Women's Army Service, yet my father, only twenty-one years old when the guns finally fell silent, was shaping fruit buns at two o'clock in the morning at Portwine's Bakery in Kalamunda. We never spoke of it. Ever. Was there a hint of disapproval or even dishonour – that a fit young bloke did not ship out from Fremantle with thousands of others? Am I dishonouring him by speculating about it? I will never know the answer.

In the 1950s, Dad drove trucks from Welshpool in Perth across the country to Sydney and back – happiest perhaps to be on the road and alone.

He married Mum, but only after she'd previously called off the engagement because she thought he drank too much and was filled with unspoken sorrows.

None of which twelve-year-old me knew anything about on that breathless summer afternoon when I posed that naive question. 'Are you happy, Dad?' Nor was I mature enough to see that he did take a moment to reflect on the enormity and complexity of it. And then he simply answered truthfully and in the negative. And walked off.

~

Today, as I write this, I am approaching my sixtieth birthday. I have walked away from a forty-year career in media and currently have my right arm in a sling following shoulder surgery. I am getting older and less relevant. I am losing power and status in a fast-changing world, and everything I know about being a bloke is now being scrutinised.

Such an appraisal is timely and important. I do not fear it. Gender equity reappraisals are overdue, and the lazy assumptions and advantages and unrealistic expectations we blokes carry with us are being revealed as just that. I welcome it. But I'm also intrigued about how we are meant to respond.

For the last few years, I've been an ambassador for the Fathering Project, a brilliant initiative designed to promote the role of dads at the heart of family life. It invites fathers to look beyond their traditional responsibilities as breadwinners and encourages them to more actively participate in their kids' lives. To be there for that Saturday-morning ballet concert. To engage. And to get the vacuum cleaner out without expecting a round of applause when it happens.

To me, there is nothing wrong in asking us to be better men and better fathers and set better examples for our kids – so our sons and daughters know what it is to be a good man. What it takes to be a good man.

Back in 2019, I presented a series of public conversations with groups of young fathers to explore how they saw their place in a changing world. I called it, 'How are you, Dad?'

And in high-school classrooms across Perth, perhaps at the behest of partners or with curiosity of their own, the dads considered the question and, after a few beers to ease the nerves, the words began to pour forth. It became very evident to me how many of them seemed unsure of the role they were meant to be playing. Perhaps even what kind of man they were expected to be.

Yes, they were freed perhaps from the rigidity of the reliable and predictable framework that had underpinned their old man's life, but they were unsure what was replacing it. And they also acknowledged that now – in their late thirties and early forties, with kids either in or about to go off to high school – they were often feeling increasingly anxious and uncertain about the role they played at home and at work.

Breadwinners still?

Practical problem-solvers?

Resilient men without fears?

Men meant to absorb life, but not reveal when it made them scared or sad or just bloody grumpy?

Men just like their dad?

Quite a few told me they did not want to be like their dad. And it wasn't because they didn't love and respect him. They just didn't want to live such prescribed lives. They wanted to be happier. To explore what that meant and if the journey was even possible.

~

A few years on and I remain fascinated and, in some ways, vexed by the challenges we blokes face. And I want to explore why so many of us succumb to a narrow and negative view of the world as we get older. Why some of us lose our curiosity and sometimes our kindness. And why, despite so many evident advantages, we can sometimes feel so thwarted and alone. Fatigued and fed up.

I keep hearing arguments that men today are in crisis, and I want to better understand if this is true.

Do we – you and me – care enough at this stage in our grand adventures to pause for some self-reflection? Allow some vulnerability to escape? And are we open to the possibility of getting better at life? Maybe adapting a little, or moving the dial of an entrenched opinion, just a fraction, to allow space for others?

I think we should try.
Are men in crisis?
You tell me.
We might even have a hug later.

Chapter 2

Does This Make You Grumpy?

I reckon I know what you're thinking. Is this the start of some long lecture about what bastards we men are? Does this bloke want to help me out, or is he just a sanctimonious, almond-milk-latte-drinking wanker?

Well, no.

I'm just trying to stretch the canvas upon which we are painting this little narrative.

And I like writing short sentences.

And asking questions, to keep you involved.

So let's get back to the question of why so many blokes seem so bloody grumpy.

All humans get grumpy. Always have done. Ever since we chimps first emerged from the primordial ooze, took a whiff of the world around us and realised our time here would probably be very brief and very brutal and smell absolutely terrible. I'm not an anthropologist, but I assume that as life's challenges dawned upon us, that's when we started flinging poo at each other.

Two million years ago, there were barely enough monkeys to fill a barrel. Today there are nearly 8.2 billion of us. And the modern world is full to bursting with individuals and interactions to be annoyed by and aggrieved about. And poo flinging? Well, life can sure give us the shits.

What exactly am I talking about?

Well, how about I throw in a few grumpy, grievance-filled examples? And perhaps you might find a pen and paper and compile a quick list of your own. We can share our gripes. I might even ask you to read them aloud with bouzouki music playing in the background, in the hope you start laughing and realise what a bloody miserable git you and I and we can sometimes be.

And who knows, we might then decide to try a bit harder to offer our families and the wider world a more adorable version of ourselves. Maybe even a tolerant one.

Deal?

So, before we make that list, let's consider what triggers our grumpiness. Or the prospect of it. Is it something occasional? A moment of frustration that suddenly inflames us? Injustice? Unfairness? Selfishness?

Maybe a scenario like this? Imagine you are out shopping – grudgingly, of course – with your partner and you notice the woman in front of you at the express checkout has maybe fifteen items in her basket, rather than the stipulated 'ten items or less'. Do you ...

a. Not care at all.
b. Sigh and mutter. And then do it repeatedly, and louder each time.
c. Start to count out each item as they are priced and offer commentary. 'There goes the second can of tuna ...'
d. Explode with anger and tell the woman she is wilfully flouting what

is surely one of life's most fundamental instructions and 'God Help Us All' if the rest of the world was as bloody selfish as she is.

Now, if your answer is anything other than (a.) then you are just looking for trouble, aren't you?

You live with the expectation that you are about to be assailed, over and over again, by other people and their sheer selfish stupidity? That's it, isn't it? THEIR STUPIDITY! And the accumulation of it. Every day. On your strong, broad, but now frankly increasingly weary shoulders.

I get it.

The world is an imperfect place. Sometimes it doesn't work the way we would like it to. Sometimes it doesn't seem to work at all. And as we get older, we begin to wonder if it is ever going to be fixed.

As if life is an unfilled pothole and the bloody council won't do anything about it until someone falls over and breaks their ankle, and even then ...

I was musing about this recently on a social-media chat, when a fellow named Graham admitted feeling perpetually exasperated about the state of the world and all of us in it.

'Geoff, it's not that I'm grumpy, it's just that everyone else is so BLOODY stupid!'

Geez, Graham, everyone?

My dad would have said the same thing.

But everyone must surely include us. What if it's our behaviour that contributes to Graham's sense of dismay?

Inconceivable, isn't it? The prospect that we could ever be the reason for someone else to feel grumpy. Or that you or I could ever contribute to that giant bucket of mean and stupid.

Well, my friends, we all can. We all do.

~

A few months ago, my wife and I went to see the opera *Carmen*, spectacularly staged outdoors at the WACA Ground in Perth.

An enormous set was built in front of the Lillee-Marsh Stand. It was from here, all those years ago, that Dennis Lillee famously pushed off the sightscreen to a chorus of roaring drunks chanting 'Li-llee, Li-llee, Li-llee' and struck fear in the heart of some hapless batsman hoping to defend himself with a thin piece of wood. Tonight, it was more 'L'amour, L'amour, L'amour'.

But before we even got to 'Habanera', I noticed a couple sitting just to my left. He sour, sallow, in his seventies and she dressed up for the evening, wearing a soft blue-and-green silk dress and a faint smile, casting quick glances in his direction to take his emotional temperature. Now where had I seen that before?

He was grumbling about something and pointing to the stage, where a Noongar man was delivering a Welcome to Country. Resplendent in furs and skins, the man on stage was acknowledging this place as the home of his people.

And then the old coot couldn't help himself. 'Why,' he asked loudly enough for all those around us to hear, 'why is he wearing a watch?'

I needed to let the moment sink in.

'Why is he wearing a watch?'

I felt his wife shrink into her seat, clutch hard at her Oroton purse and stare determinedly ahead. Trying not to take the bait.

And the old coot? Not chastened at all. He repeated the question: 'Why is he wearing a watch?'

I wanted to say something. 'Indigenous Australians wear watches too, mate.' Or, 'Maybe he wanted to know what time you'd stop being a dickhead!' But I didn't. Imagine the shame his wife would feel.

And a sullen evening, I presume, was had by all.

What a grumpy old prick.

~

(Imagine, if you will, the hands of a clock spinning wildly, or dates flying off a calendar. Perhaps even a sun setting, rising and setting again in a frantic time-lapse ...)

~

Okay, I have in recent months wanted to reappraise the Old Coot. Capital letters now I have formally named him.

Primarily because I reacted so strongly to him that night. And yes, because his behaviour was reminiscent of my dad's ability to, on occasions, spoil a family get-together with a sneering aside or a refusal to engage at all.

The question is, why on that night did Old Coot choose to present himself to the world that way? Confronting, negative and deeply unpleasant, presumably in the company of the person he most loved. Or had once.

It's easy not to care, but how else do we understand grumpiness if we don't ask where it comes from?

'Why is he wearing a watch?'

Was Old Coot a racist? And proudly so? Was he questioning the appropriateness of a Noongar man welcoming him to his own country?

Had he not wanted to come to the opera anyway, and was this a way of chastising his wife for refusing to let him stay at home?

Or ... and perhaps this is unlikely ... was he once an aspiring baritone? Was it Young Coot who, playing Escamillo the Toreador on opening night of *Carmen* at the Albany Town Hall in 1971, forgot to be forever on his guard and fell off the stage and into the lap of the lord mayor's wife? Never to sing in public again.

I don't know.

But I do know that how we present ourselves to the world today has a hell of a lot to do with what came before. And like Old Coot and my dad and possibly yours and possibly you, we may choose never to share that with others.

We may not want to. We may not know how to. We may be scared to. We must be forever on our guard.

And the consequence may well be that our wives and partners and kids, despite their best efforts to understand, can never get quite close enough to help us out. Because we don't want them to know us. We don't want them to think us weak. Or vulnerable.

Better that we reveal nothing of our fragility or fear or sense of failure or shame. Better we explain nothing and apologise for nothing. Better we barge on, decrying other people as stupid.

Better we just remain grumpy and fling our metaphorical poo.

~

Is it better, though?

It seems to me that when exposed to the stupidity of the world around us, we do have options.

We can simply let things go. How's that for a statement of the bleeding obvious?

Does it really matter if the woman in front of us in the ten-items-or-less queue has fifteen items in her basket?

Or ...

We can arm ourselves with anger and contempt and righteousness and hoard those grievances. Maybe even curate a collection of stupidity that validates everything we think about this very stupid world. Our Museum of Dickheadedness.

The problem is, that museum, filled with display cases of the foolish and fatuous, is housed in our guts and presents only as a malignant stew, a great gastric unhappiness, the vapours of which seep into all parts of our lives and relationships and if unchecked will simply destroy our capacity for joy.

For joy.

I think curating exhibits of other people's stupidity is a miserable, self-defeating and often self-pitying hobby.

So if you're thinking of opening such a museum, bloody don't.

~

Here's the question I will ask again and again. Can you imagine what life might be like, if we – me and you – consciously tried to pull back a little when annoyed or aggrieved?

To not feel the urge to judge so quickly, or find fault, or lay blame. Or offer such a loud opinion. Or correct. Or need to be right. All the time.

What if we just allowed some of that frustration to pass? Recognising the idiocy of it perhaps, but not becoming a lightning rod for it. Aware of it but determined not to be overwhelmed by it.

How do we do that?

Well, I think we have to agree on something. We have to accept the premise that it is not inevitable for men to become grumpy as we get older.

Why do I believe this? Because I see blokes celebrating life every day. Being tender and kind to those they love most, and obliging and friendly to those they might have just met.

I saw a great example of it this morning at the beach, ahead of a brutally hot day. An older chap was playing with his granddaughter, who looked to be about seven or eight. They were eating Twisties. He was tentatively presenting them, the way you might offer a seagull a chip. She leant in, laughing every time. Occasionally he would pull away and she would snatch at empty air.

He then tilted his head, lifted the bag to his mouth and emptied the dregs, making appropriately grotesque noises. She feigned outrage. Encouraged by this, he pulled something moist and yellow from inside his gob and offered it to her by way of apology.

'You're disgusting,' she cried.

'I know,' he replied, before chasing her to the shoreline as she made her escape into the sparkling blue water.

I don't know that bloke, but I liked the sound of his laugh and the apparent ease of his relationship with his granddaughter. And there's a pretty good chance that, thirty or forty years from now, the grown woman will remember him, for his love and his kindness and his sense of mischief.

My father-in-law did it with lolly snakes and my adult kids have never forgotten.

~

If this book is to resonate with you in any way, then I think we have to agree there are more laughs to be had, more tender moments to share and more wonderful memories to build and bank.

Can we agree on that? Do I have to fling poo at you or tousle your hair, just to piss you off enough to get a nod of agreement?

Good. Then it's settled.

~

Now, lest you think I am just some sanctimonious, smug, do-gooding, former ABC, politically correct, too-woke-by-half wanker ... well, you'd be partly right. I did just use the word 'lest' after all ...

But I do want you to know that I am exploring the 'grumpy phenomenon' not to sneer at you or tease you or anger you, but to share this adventure with you. I don't want to be sucked into the vortex of endless harrumphing either. It's fucking grim. And I, like you, am just as vulnerable to it.

Indeed, last weekend, as I read the local rag, which featured something I didn't agree with, I immediately set my 'I've Never Been So Outraged' meter to eleven and declared to anyone who would listen ...

'I'll write to the bloody paper about this!'

No one was listening.

And I huffed and puffed and began to dictate my anger into the air. Indulging my urgent need to correct. To put the bastards straight. To feel empowered again, in a world gone mad.

Anyway, I was clearly about to do all those things (not sure how), when I noticed a look of concern and some disappointment on the face of my wife (at this point I give myself some credit for having enough self-awareness to sense I was about to be ludicrous).

'Are you really going to become the angry man in the newspaper?' she asked, presumably preparing herself for another thirty years of opinionated tedium or to consider whether it might be an opportune time to grab the car keys and bolt. 'Perhaps they can send a photographer around and you can pose with a furrowed brow and folded arms.'

She was right, of course. I didn't really want to become Angry Man in the local paper. Annoyed by life's potholes and demanding to know when council would fix them to my satisfaction.

I let it go.

It took some effort.

(No, it didn't. I just had to swallow some of my self-important stupidity.)

And much of what I'm about to ask you is about your capacity to let things go.

~

Shall we do a little test of your tolerance? Ascertain your capacity for outrage or your willingness to just shrug and move on?

Let's consider some of the issues in life that make us grumpy, and you can either sit there seething with incandescent, heart-attack-inducing rage … or perhaps you can wave away these exhibits of idiocy, allowing them to slide harmlessly by before crashing into the next bloke, who you can watch with detached amusement become all red-faced and cranky.

(Perhaps we need the bouzouki music from the Monty Python Cheese Shop sketch to set the mood. 'Da, da, da, dum, da dum, da dum …')

- Let's say it begins with something you saw on the *Today* show this morning about lines of people queuing in Midland so they can be the first to eat at a new Taco Bell. What a low-bar claim to fame. Queuing for a quesadilla. People these days etc., etc. ...
- And of course you've already had a run-in with Mrs Drobny, the old Czech woman next door with the moustache, whose bloody Lhasa Apso never lets up with its confounded yap, yap, yapping when she's at work. How many times have you wondered about throwing a bait over the fence and seeing what happens?
- And what about that nitwit driver in the white Camry who just came to a complete halt at a green light because of an overabundance of caution, forcing you to hit the skids? And now it's turned red and he has blithely sailed through.
- And hang on, what did that cricket commentator on the radio just say about the peculiar superstition of umpire Dickie Bird, where he'd stand on one foot whenever the score reached 111? It wasn't Dickie Bird; it was David Shepherd.

   Get your facts right!

   Get your facts right, world!

   Why doesn't anyone know anything anymore?

   Why are people so stupid?

~

Let's do a test, not a real one.

No prizes, just a means of taking the temperature of your brain.

Think of it as a word-association fireworks display. I want to know what explodes and fizzes within you.

Ready?

Here we go – images off the top of my head. Feel free to add your own. It might even make you laugh.

- Every motorist who is not you. Those arsehats who don't know the etiquette of the roundabout, or how to indicate, or merge, or drive at an appropriate speed in the right-hand lane, or tow a caravan properly, and certainly can't reverse into the allocated space next to your berth, or secure their tent pegs (that'll be fun when the wind whips up later tonight), or keep their bloody kids quiet after eight o'clock as is designated on the Happy Wanderer Caravan Park noticeboard, which they might have seen when they came in were they not bickering quite so loudly. Look at the state of them. And who cut that kid's hair?

    You conclude, not unreasonably, that they are probably drug users or Sovereign Citizens or Greens voters or all of the above.

- Any reality-TV program – but particularly *Love Island* – although you did say to your daughter when she dropped in last week after netball that you wouldn't mind watching an updated version of *Gilligan's Island* where Little Buddy did finally get it off with Ginger. You thought that was hilarious. She thought you were having a stroke.

    And what about *Farmer Wants a Wife*? 'No, he doesn't,' you shout at the telly. 'He just wants someone to give him a bloody hand with the mulesing.'

- Then of course there are those god-awful cooking shows. Tonight's signature dish is … 'Rissoles!' you bellow at the screen.

'Who watches this rubbish?' you ask repeatedly.

'The young people,' says your wife, unless she's gone to book club, which she increasingly wishes was on every night.

- Have you tried to buy razor blades lately? Bewildering. They're usually called The Platinum This or The Mach That and are presumably designed by Lockheed Martin and endorsed by racing-car drivers or cricketers with sharp jawlines who look very, very pleased with themselves for having learnt how to shave.

  Trawl the aisle looking for a simple blade to cut your old white whiskers and you'll instead be offered a turbo, 3D, extra-lubed, anti-friction, pro-shield, skin-guard system featuring cool cartridge technology and an exfoliating bar so you can shave your balls.

  The price, like the ball-shaving technology, is eye-watering, and you still have no idea if it will fit your razor.

  Anyway ... on we go.

- Do you remember when you used to be able to rely on the ABC? Sensible newsreaders (usually men) giving you the facts. Now they keep telling you what you can and can't say and how you mustn't offend people who want to identify as bees or sausages (vegan only, please).

  Truth is, the older we get, the less we understand – anything.

- What are social influencers anyway? You're not even sure what the phrase means, but it seems to relate to bulbous-bottomed young women – who may or may not have been created by AI – selling other people the benefits of something called mindfulness. Yesterday I heard that some style icon was trying to sell beer made from vaginal yeast. Anyway, as you understand it, they mainly ply their trade on

TikTok and YouTube, which you don't really know much about either, although you have enjoyed watching repeats of *The World at War* when the rest of the house has gone quiet.

Or gone out.

- The Kardashians? It all seems so vacuous. The relentless selling of 'You too can be like me' dreams to silly, self-centred, lip-plumped narcissists who are convinced this banal rubbish represents a profound 21st-century cultural truth.

And yes, while we can concede the odd point – we're not unreasonable – and do understand that perhaps these influencers are changing the consumer habits of a new generation, it does make the rest of us hanker for simpler times. In our house, for instance, mindfulness for Dad represented twenty uninterrupted minutes on the toilet with the paper every morning, before one of us kids knocked on the door and declared we were 'busting!'

That's right, we only had one toilet. Tell that to the kids today.

~

Let me offer a few more itches to scratch:

- People who stop just as they are about to step off an escalator.
- Anyone who wants you to take off your shoes when you enter their homes.
- Plant-based ham.
- Every single thing about going to Officeworks.
- Any suggestion at all that we have achieved 'synergy'.
- The private equity firms that own the pet-care industry and think it's

okay to charge twenty-five dollars for a dog's heartworm tablet. How much do we love our pets? Don't push me.
- Anyone who declares they are on a 'journey' or has 'a story'.
- The barista who demands your name even when you are the only person in the cafe and then still looks past you and calls out, 'Macchiato for Tom?'
- Baristas? My arse.
- Any media appearance by politicians who declare their concern for people 'doing it tough'.
- Fridges that feature television screens.
- Beer made from fruit. And the people that buy it.
- The unsolicited automated phone call on the landline demanding we make an erroneous eBay payment.
- Australia Post delivering an item – usually late – and then emailing and asking in a folksy tone, 'How'd we do?' As if it's their first day delivering things.
- The current-affairs promo that warns this is 'a story no parent can afford to miss'.

    And ...
- The fact that Benny Hill and every other comedian you ever liked appear to have been cancelled by the woke police.

    Whoever they are.

So there we are. Just a few exhibits, mind. Just a random sample of the inconsequential. Unless it's not inconsequential to you.

How many of them make you grumpy? How many more can you come up with? Can I suggest you add to them?

I'm serious. Why not make your own list? Yes, I'm looking at you, fella. Why not spend fifteen minutes accumulating grievances? Piling them high on a plate of discontent. No annoyance too trite.

And then, while imagining you are hearing that bouzouki music in the background, read them out aloud.

I bet you start to laugh.

'Da, da, da, dum, da dum, da dum ...'

- Restaurant waitstaff who manage to walk past tables completely oblivious to anyone seeking to catch their eye.
- Daughter's boyfriend who says he is perpetually exhausted yet appears to do nothing much at all.
- Anyone who wants to 'reach out'.
- Or 'value-add'.
- Or 'circle back'.
- The dentist strongly suggesting it's time for a crown, when we both know he just wants me to help fund his next ski holiday to Val d'Isère.

'Da, da, da, dum, da dum, da dum ...'

Give it a try. Go hard. You may be surprised how refreshed you feel.

It might even be a mindfulness thing. Like sitting on the toilet with the paper.

~

And so I ask again. How many of those grievances are you determined to hold onto and what might you be prepared to just let go?

I, for instance, don't care if I never see another episode of *The Benny*

Hill Show, although I did quite admire the sheer nerve of basing every joke around time-lapse 'Yakety Sax' sketches featuring revolting old men chasing near-naked nurses.

What I'd love you to at least consider over the following pages is whether the accumulation of annoyance and exasperation, complaints and pet hates (or hate of other people's pets) is really making you happy.

Or more RIGHT.

Or more VALIDATED.

Or more IN CONTROL.

Or more HAPPY.

And yes, I repeated that because it matters.

Or is it simply making you, and those who float within your angry orbit, more MISERABLE?

Perhaps you think this is nonsense. That I am catastrophising the impact of this kind of behaviour.

The relentless appraisal and criticism and correction of everything. The mistakes latched onto and corrected. The weaknesses in others poked at. Every single day.

After all, it's not your fault you are exact and have high standards.

Well, let me be frank, I reckon, you and I, we are risking plenty, if this is how we now communicate with and assess the world. Such miserable fault-finding righteousness is very, *very* bad for our health and happiness. And if it doesn't kill us, it will, in all likelihood, begin to isolate us.

And at some point, our partners will notice but not alert us to the fact – lest they threaten our fragile sense of self – that the grandkids aren't quite so keen on a sleepover anymore.

Or that the young fella can't really be bothered to come home for

Friday-night pizza and footy. Because you keep going on about players' haircuts.

Truth is, the possible consequence of a world without you, me or us actively playing a positive role in it might just be a funeral where, with nothing much to eulogise, Father Ted will have no option but to pluck, seemingly from nowhere, that 'Bob, of course, loved his snooker'.

Even though it was Bob being remembered yesterday and your name is Terry.

~

At this point, you are perhaps looking at your partner. The person who saw this book in WH Smith at the airport and thrust it in your lap, just moments before you boarded a flight to Sydney to see your daughter and son-in-law.

He, by the way, is a big-noting bullshit artist you can't stand – and despite the appeals of your wife to just this once try to ignore his boastful ways, you have no intention of doing so.

But may there be pause for thought. May you ponder for just one moment ...

Why did she buy this book for me?

And you will either choose to feel, as you so often do, under attack. Or you may soften a little, look into her eyes, however briefly, and see that perhaps you are the source of the tension today. And most days.

Except on Thursdays when you play golf. And even then, if you've had a few beers, you become belligerent.

So what do you want to do?

Can you acknowledge that maybe you do risk losing touch with those around you a little? That you might actually be making yourself and others unhappy?

My dad was aware of the impact of his behaviour, but the best he could ever come up with was, 'I'm sorry if I ...' Which is a bit pissant.

~

Do you want things to change?

Well, for Dad it took a while. He seemed unwilling and incapable of escaping his circumstance, and it meant that for years Mum walked around on eggshells so as not to upset the delicate equilibrium of each day in retirement. I have read her diaries and have to admit that my dad, through much of his sixties and seventies, could be petulant and childish. And she would compromise her day almost every day to ensure there was peace and calm. As women do.

And yet, and to his credit, as Dad aged, he grew tired, I think, of being so righteous and negative and judgemental and grumpy. Fed up perhaps with being fed up. Even exhausted by it. And his kind heart began to beat again.

And today my kids remember him with great and real love. That was his belated gift to us. It is an enduring one.

What would you like to leave behind?

Chapter 2 and a Bit

Why I Love Being a Bloke

Before we go any further, I'd like to share with you just one of the many reasons I am grateful to be a bloke.

It's all explained by a social-media video that was doing the rounds a few years ago. It shows two little boys, probably five or six years old, one wearing an orange T-shirt, the other a green one. They are both in shorts and barefoot. They look similar. They may be brothers. They are standing next to a pedal bin, which comes up to their chests.

One positions himself behind it and leans in, to face his unknown destiny. The other presses the pedal with his foot. The bin lid rears up on its hinge and smacks the first boy in the face with a sharp, percussive snap.

The action is repeated.

They then swap places, so the head-injured boy can now inflict a similar punishment on his mate.

Snap!

There is laughter and anticipation and shock and just a hint of fear about the action and its inevitable consequences. There is no lesson learnt. They are having too much fun.

Snap!

And it's a fantastic reminder of how inventive and curious and just plain dumb we can be. And how much pleasure we take from it.

And if we made someone else laugh, even better.

Please continue ...

Chapter 3

Thinking About Retirement

Over the next few years, it's estimated there will be more than five million Australians living in retirement of some form. Five million of us! That's a lot of people queuing at cafes asking for a 'piping hot' cappuccino and for the music to be turned down.

For many of us, retirement will represent golden years of opportunity and enjoyment where, released from the responsibility of work and raising families, we can now choose to either stop and smell the roses or boldly embark on new adventures ...

I think we can also safely assume there are probably going to be many, many retired men who don't have very much to do.

With all that time.

Now they've read the paper.

Listened to a bit of talkback radio.

Watered the garden.

Or, rather miserably, followed wives or partners to the supermarket and, in lieu of actually helping, chosen to plonk down on the padded bench out the front and wait. Or doze off. With mouth open. Only to be roused by the anxious query of a worried little boy to his mum: 'Mummy, is that man dead?'

Apologies for having a crack at clichés and stereotypes. Please see them for the caricatures they are. Please do not look in the mirror and think that caricature resembles you.

But we have seen those blokes down the shops, right? And we have laughed at them a bit, haven't we? And we have said or thought to ourselves, 'I hope I don't end up like that.' Haven't we?

~

So let's talk about your retirement.

How much thought have you given it, beyond playing out the conversation with your boss and inviting him to go and fuck himself?

Or the fantasy of sitting in that last strategy meeting and suggesting to Tiffany, the head of HR, that today's cupcake morning tea was not so much designed to bring the world together as one as to provide her with the opportunity to post a picture on LinkedIn and be affirmed by other Tiffanys in other HR departments for caring so much about clubfooted dolphins or whatever was next on the list of endangered, traumatised and bullied things that requires us to publicly state our support while determinedly doing absolutely nothing practical, feasible or sincere to help them.

How many times did you wish you'd say that? Knowing also that to do so might mean you would face a formal tut-tutting censure for not being collaborative enough and, quite possibly, accusations of workplace harassment.

Frankly, sometimes we just need to know when it's time to go.

Truth is, the manner in which we bid farewell to a lifetime of full-time work is usually determined one of three ways.

We reach the retirement age and become eligible for our superannuation. Goodbye, boss. Farewell, Tiffany.

We retire because of ill health or disability. Sorry about that angry prostate, Brian. Good luck.

Or someone else decides we are retiring. Our contract is not renewed; we are retrenched or sacked. Did you hear about Sanjeep? Poor bastard didn't see that coming.

Our decision to retire is not always ours. We are often funnelled towards it. And that means when it arrives, we are not always prepared for one of the great structural changes of our lives.

That is what it is: a great structural change. Ten, twenty, maybe thirty years of life ahead without full-time work. And possibly without a sense of purpose.

~

Consider the scope of that challenge for a moment. If we can't reconcile or see opportunity with that new version of ourselves, then the last years of our lives might be very long and very grumpy indeed.

It does, of course, depend on the circumstances of your farewell. Go on your own terms and there is potential for great personal satisfaction.

When I hung up my headphones at ABC Radio in November 2022, a twenty-four-year career at the national broadcaster and more than forty years in the media came to an end. And I was very privileged. It finished indulgently. A studio audience stood and applauded as I bade them 'Hoo Roo' for the last time. They seemed to like me well enough and were broadly sorry I was leaving.

It was a far cry from the day we first met, back in June 2006, when, within minutes of turning on my microphone, I received a text message from an audience member who asked, 'Who's this fucking dipstick?'

Who indeed?

'Hoo Roo' was something my dad and his generation said. And at the end of that first day on air, it was a farewell I offered more by accident than design. I was exhausted and had frankly run out of anything else to say.

'Hoo Roo,' I said, barely expecting to be invited back.

I was invited back. And it stuck. I said it every day for the next sixteen years.

Goodbye. Thanks.

I never even really knew how to spell it. Like 'Uh Oh'.

And there I was in 2022, having said a final 'Hoo Roo' and barely realising that I was about to step into the sticky aspic of 'Uh Oh'.

'Uh Oh'. What just happened?

And what happens next?

In the weeks that followed, I felt relief and pleasure and some confusion. Discombobulated by the word 'retirement': a word I now despise.

And I pondered just how often over the years I'd talked to the ABC Radio audience about what happens when full-time work finishes and we transition into ... what exactly? We'd spoken regularly of the need to recognise that significant change is coming. And, with it, endless, often daunting questions to consider.

Do you have enough money? What will it be like to not go to work each day? Will you miss the status you enjoyed? The banter of your colleagues? Will you be able to find a new routine? Doing what?

Will it feel like a luxuriously soft breeze of infinite possibility? Or will all those unscheduled hours rub you raw and restless?

What will you do?

What will you do?

What will you do?

This is looking and sounding a bit like a Dr Seuss book, isn't it?

The Cat in the Hat Gets Sacked.

And then we begin to ponder these huge questions based on our limited observation of other retired people. Or Dad and Mum. Is there really contentment to be found in pruning roses and having a well-kept lawn?

Or maybe I could become like my neighbour Helmut, who, as I write this, is playing Horst Jankowski's 'A Walk in the Black Forest' on the piano. He is not so much tinkling the ivories as clubbing them with truncheons of bratwurst. It may not be beautiful to listen to, but the intent is glorious. Helmut is clearly having the time of his life. He is doing something he loves to do.

And all of us share his desire to get better at it. Dear God, please.

So while we consider what we might do next, Helmut's approach is quite appealing. If you like something, pursue it, and have as much fun as you can along the way.

Rose pruning? Piano playing? Are they even worse clichés than the one I just threw at you about sitting asleep, mouth agape, in a shopping centre?

What do we really know of this transition before we make it?

In my case, not much.

I told everyone I'd enjoy a summer in the People's Republic of South Fremantle, maybe do some travel and then consider what comes next in the back half of the following year. It sounded like a plan. It was also a way of avoiding further enquiry. It would buy me some time.

And, frankly, I found the well-intended 'But what will you DO?' question relentless and a bit irritating. It was such an earnest interrogation of my future, as if I'd just revealed I had inoperable brain cancer or my wife had run off with a spoon salesman.

'But what will you DO?'

'Kill them both,' I thought, 'and then start on the neighbours.'

Over time, I realised the question was wrapped in the uncertainty and doubt of whoever was asking it. Their fear of a future without structure. Or maybe money. Or good health. Or happiness, whatever that may look like.

And it's true, the question of whether we can afford to retire determines the focus of most of our upcoming decisions. Stay with me on this. In the next chapter, long-time ABC *Nightlife* finance guy Nick Bruining will offer you a few things to consider on the subject of money and whether you will have enough of it. Or die penniless in the street.

But right now I want to delve into the psychology of retirement and how we might best make that transition and be satisfied by it. Or at least be aware of the pitfalls.

~

It seems to me, we simply don't give retirement enough thought. Too often it just arrives. It happens to us.

Professor Gary Martin is the CEO of the Australian Institute of Management and a workplace media commentator. He deals with this issue all the time.

I begin by asking him how many of us plan for our retirement. Or how many of us rather fall into it, probably in a state of exhaustion.

'Geoff, I think people do plan for it, but only based on their financial situation. The number-one factor will be, "Can I afford to retire?" and that's a prerequisite for many people. But beyond that, many people don't think through what retirement represents. So, for example, if you don't have any hobbies or interests prior to retiring, if you have lived to work, then you better start to plan for some, because you'll end up isolated and grumpy if you've got nothing to do.'

Isolated and grumpy.

With nothing to do.

We want to avoid that at all costs.

So telling the boss what you really think of him or questioning Tiffany's motivation for Cupcake Tuesday might be part of the fantasy finish of a working life, but it won't prepare you for Day 1 or Day 35 or Day 678 of the aftermath. That will be up to you.

Experience tells Gary that our first couple of months or perhaps even year of retirement might pass easily enough. There are Friday lunches to be enjoyed and maybe that long-awaited overseas holiday. There is the luxury and novelty of doing nothing. Or having nothing you have to do.

Imagine that. The pleasure of only being accountable to yourself. Go on, ask yourself, 'How would I like to fill my day today?'

Now imagine asking yourself that question every day.

Personally, I bloody love it, but I am still basking in the novelty of not going to strategy meetings with Tiffany.

If most of your social interactions have relied on relationships established at work, or if your partner is still employed and has a very organised routine of their own, who are you going to enjoy the luxury of doing nothing with? The dog? He's just wandered outside to lick his bits. He doesn't want another walk.

~

Just be aware too that later on in this chapter I will be asking you more questions about your partner, and what their aspirations might be. At that point, you'll also hear the sound of an air-raid siren going off, so maybe go and get a glass of water.

~

Gary Martin reckons there are three questions you and I need to consider.

Just a warning. There are a lot more than three questions.

'First up, Geoff, "What am I going to do to find structure in my day?"' It's an obvious question, because you can't sit around and listen to the races or watch the cricket all day. What routines am I going to establish to put meaning into that day?

'The second one is, "What am I going to do to get me thinking and engaging?" What do I do to remain curious? What skills do I have to offer my community? What new ones might I like to learn?

'And then the third one, obviously, is, "What am I going to do to boost my friendship circles?" Because friendship circles just deplete after retirement. How will I invest in them?'

There's a lot to consider there, Gary. And we have to take each question seriously. All eight of them.

You may hope, with a shoulder shrug, that somehow they will take care of themselves, but they won't. Look at them again. We have to see the opportunity here. And if you are lucky enough to have the reassurance of financial security, then you should start to consider another gift you have been given.

It is the gift of time.

And you might be a bit rusty about how you choose to use it, because most of those hours have been allocated to work and family life for the last forty years. But that is about to change. Now you have a lot of time on your hands to panel-beat the piano keys as Helmut does so enthusiastically. You have a lot of time on your hands to improve a golf swing and get good exercise. You have a lot of time on your hands to go and cook breakfast on a Monday morning for members of your community who sleep rough.

And here's one I particularly like ...

You have a lot of time on your hands to indulge the memory of things you liked to do as a kid and probably abandoned once the task of being a responsible adult took over. This offers both nostalgia and opportunity. We get to indulge the memory and we also get to live the pleasure of the experience again.

~

When I was twelve and imagining what my adult life might look like, I hoped there would be room for a game of tennis every day. I loved it.

Australia had such a rich history of success in the sport, and the ice-and-fire rivalry between Björn Borg and John McEnroe had made it ever more compelling. Using Mum's old Slazenger Challenge, I'd hit forehands against a tired timber backboard at the Kalamunda Tennis Club, dreaming that one day John Newcombe might just happen to drive by, take an interest and invite me to join the Davis Cup team. At twelve.

Newk never came, and I didn't play Davis Cup tennis for Australia.

And as years passed, I didn't play much tennis at all. When I did step onto a court, my once-big serve dissolved into embarrassment. I'd compensate for a lack of practice by overreaching and refusing to play the percentages. I repeatedly dragged those serves into the net or hit them absurdly long, and failure became self-fulfilling.

I found reasons not to play. The racquet went into the shed. Didn't matter. I had other things to do.

Well, a couple of months ago, a friend invited me to come and have a hit with some of his mates. I really wanted to. I then tried to find reasons why I shouldn't.

Beware. This can happen a lot. The reflex of saying 'no' instead of 'yes'. It's just easier somehow. Even though we fully understand a really great opportunity and genuine invitation has been extended. But we say 'no'.

Why is that? The fear of not meeting our own expectations? The fear that others will judge us and we will let them down?

Well guess what? Those others are too worried about their own serve, or their own inability to hit a backhand, to care about my or your slightly neurotic pre-game nerves. A reminder perhaps of the perils of spending too much time in our own heads wondering what other people think of us, when the reality appears to be: not much. They are too busy being in their own heads, wondering what we are thinking about them.

I did go. And while my serve was still crap and I still tried to hit my way out of my shambolic circumstances, the feel of the racquet in my hand was the handshake of an old friend. On the inside, I was twelve years old again, even if on the outside I was bloody hopeless. But unlike two hours before, that no longer mattered.

Now I want to go back. I want to have some lessons. Why wouldn't I return to one of the things I used to love to do?

And on that ...

Just a few moments ago, my sixty-five-year-old brother proudly sent me a photo of a horse float he's bought and the second-hand Cuban-heeled RM Williams boots he intends to wear.

Pete, as a teenager, was a very keen horseman, like our dad, but opportunities to own and ride a nag all but disappeared when other life commitments rode into view. In the intervening decades, Pete has held fast to the memory and the dream of it being renewed, and a few years ago he decided the time was right to go riding again. He decided riding horses really mattered to him.

The experience has brought him not just a nice reminder of another time, but enormous and ongoing pleasure. By purchasing the float today, a new world will open up for Pete and his ten-year-old horse, Joe, to wander and discover the many and varied trails of South-East Queensland. And that's where you'll find him when he farewells work later this year.

So, obvious question. What did you like doing as a kid?

I'm not suggesting you go back to stealing lollies from Woolies or throwing eggs at the principal's office, but think hard about the hobbies and games and activities you used to love so much. Maybe you were good at them. Maybe this time around you won't be so good at them. Maybe that won't matter anymore.

You are being offered the gift of time to explore and enjoy them again. And perhaps you can use that long, languid walk around the golf course to consider what else you might like to do next. It's almost luxurious. So embrace it.

~

All of this sounds great if you, like me, have been fortunate enough to call a halt to your working life on your own terms. Where you have time to plan. Some of us aren't so lucky. Whether it's through illness or disability or redundancy or dismissal, the working lives of many Australians come to an end well before they should.

You might be a medically retired police officer or the brickie whose spine is so compressed you can barely get out of bed in the morning.

Maybe you are a suit wearer in the corporate sector and you've just been called into the big corner office to hear that the company is pursuing a 'new direction'. They are, you are told, looking to 'change gears' or 'refresh the brand', or they're 'pivoting' or embarking on an 'exciting journey of transition'. And they've decided you're not coming with them. And so they reach into a grab bag of euphemistic phrases designed to disguise the reality that you are being sacked, retrenched, dismissed or made redundant. Sometimes it comes with apology and regret and a generous farewell. Sometimes it comes with a security guard escorting you to the car park before you can even say goodbye to your colleagues.

This is an altogether different introduction to retirement.

And it can be a fragile time.

I've asked a very good friend of mine, Michael, to talk a little about his experience with a forced redundancy. He too was simply told that his services were no longer required. He too was tipped into a retirement for which he was unprepared.

Michael and I have a unique friendship. We were work colleagues, albeit in different states for many years. And our friendship was built on the telephone.

Some twenty years later, we still ring each other every Friday afternoon and shoot the breeze. We talk nonsense. We talk about real life. And we each benefit from the ability of the other to be a careful and thoughtful listener.

Michael and I have not met face to face more than half a dozen times over the course of our friendship. It doesn't matter. We know each other well.

First up – Michael, thank you for talking about this. I remember when it happened. I remember how quietly shaken you were. But I don't think, even now, I know the extent to which it impacted your life. Can you take me back to those days?

'Geoff, the career that I had enjoyed for more than thirty years ended just months before I turned fifty-five. Over the years, I thought I had done okay. I worked for some big organisations and was in a senior role where, among other things, I was mentoring young colleagues. I was one of about twenty-four people made redundant. Later, our positions were renamed and given to younger staff members.

'What came first? I think it was a deep sense of humiliation. The awkward conversations. Having to sign the papers up against a wall, because all the HR hot desks were being used. The excruciating final morning tea and card ceremony. Handing in my security pass. Strangely, I took a photo of my old pigeonhole. And then I left.

'And the farewell? There was an evening of bravado at the local pub before people slipped off, knowing they had a busy weekend ahead, before going back to work on Monday.'

Michael, the guest of honour, sat through a few hours of this, knowing he would not be joining them. He was not being invited back.

I want to know how he felt. Was he numb? Disappointed but accepting? Or was he furious? My friend is usually a taciturn sort of fellow.

'The crankiness arrived quickly. In my head, conversations were replayed, perceived injustices revisited, and I scrambled to find the moral high ground.

'Then came the sadness and the feeling that perhaps I had been a bit shit at the job and that maybe people had worn fake smiles, all the while hoping this bloke would be moved on soon.

'The final iteration was detachment. Nothing mattered, and if I went for a long walk in the bush one day and never returned, it wouldn't affect anyone's life.'

Michael didn't think he mattered anymore. And he has just revealed how vulnerable he was and we are, when so much of our self-worth is derived from our workplace and what happens when that identity and status is taken from us. And yes, it does sound very much as if he was experiencing the oft-quoted five stages of grief.

Michael, what happened next? Was it acceptance?

'It was odd. I didn't miss work, but I missed the purpose of it, and being a little short financially of where I needed to be, I began to scout around. Kind people told me "you will be snapped up" and that my phone would run hot. The phone was so quiet I once checked it in case I'd accidently switched it off. Job applications went unanswered. One old colleague asked me to come in for a chat, and when I arrived for the appointment, I was told he was in Sydney that week.

'Then came a position I was very keen on. A new role in an organisation I greatly admired. I more than had the requisite experience, and the more I read about it, the more fresh ideas popped into my head. After two days working on an application and preparing for an interview, I emailed it for the Friday deadline. The robotic email rejection came at 9.01 Monday morning.

'Someone told me many companies use an AI program to filter applications, with date of birth being the first culling point. This happened so often that I stopped applying. No one wants to hire their dad.'

What a telling observation. And a bloody sad one. Ageism is alive and well and, despite many voices of dismay, continues to undermine and devalue the Australian workplace.

And these days, if your CV doesn't contain the required buzzwords that match the skills and competencies listed in the job ad, there's every chance it will not even be seen. An algorithm will call, 'Next!'

Feeling like the unemployable dad, Michael took up an offer from a retired work colleague and went and played golf instead. It gave him time and space to think.

'We hadn't had a hit for years and so we muddled our way about. Often our conversation drifted into grizzling about the old workplace, but that coincided with Titleist balls being savagely sliced out of bounds. Without ever articulating it, we both realised reopening those wounds was bad for our golf and therefore bad for us. We stopped it. We still play every fortnight, and I am always grateful for his call. It was the start of a rebalance.'

Michael needed to work, and there were a series of short-term jobs. He didn't mind. He had no option but to accept this very different work status.

'You were not who you used to be; you were just someone who could do a job. It was unexpectedly liberating. Others had been through the same experience as me, and we laughed in the tearoom and shrugged our shoulders and got paid. The months became years, and today it feels like forever since I was booted out.'

Earlier in this chapter, I talked about the gift of time available to us when we leave work. A gift or a curse. Again, that is entirely up to us. I'm interested to know how Michael sees this.

'The biggest question when leaving work is what you will do with your time, because something that was scarce is now abundant. Putting a value on it helped. This is a currency that can be spent, so what are we buying with it? The catch-up coffees with old workmates, where they felt the need to tell me how lucky I was to not be at work, became, frankly, tedious. I wanted to do new things because I could not stand the company of that chorus anymore.

'I opted for more music and less talkback, more reading and less Facebook. Opportunities opened up to do things I hadn't anticipated, and following these unknown paths was rewarding. It did take practice and a bit of consciousness, but being curious and positive can be cultivated.

'Carl Jung said, "I am not what happened to me, I am what I choose to become." That feels about right, and it also helps with my putting.'

Michael has a wisdom and quiet resilience I greatly admire. And he also urged me to write this book. Always seeking the best for others. A natural mentor.

So there are the lucky among us, who get to choose when we retire and can consider our options accordingly, and there are many who have no such choice. There is also a third category.

Those of you who are still going to work every day. And absolutely love it.

And talk of retirement comes from the mouths of others.

My advice to you is simple. Don't stop. If you love it, keep doing it.

~

Now I reckon this next bit might arrive like a sharp jab to the esteem of some readers. It's about relationships. At home.

(Sorry, was that an air-raid siren going off?)

Remember that line about sitting asleep on the bench outside the supermarket while your partner does the shopping? Have you actually talked about your retirement with the person who will be most impacted by it? Your partner?

May I suggest, in the friendliest but most forthright manner possible, that you should make no assumptions about how delighted they might be to have you at home every day?

And further to that, please tell me you do not expect your partner to give up their job, just because you have chosen to do so.

Indeed, I was just reading an old *Forbes* magazine article entitled 'Why Married Men Are So Terrible at Retirement', written by a sage fellow named Robert Laura. He contends that when men retire, we assume things will go a certain way. And that means our way. Robert Laura argues that married men need to understand that our partner may not want to share our retirement dream.

'Yes, you've worked hard and sacrificed a lot to get here, but you didn't do it solo and 10 times out of 10, married men are only as good as the spouse they have beside them. If you can't grasp this "we" concept, the chances of you becoming a gray divorce statistic dramatically increases ...'

Is he right? It is true that as we dream of escaping the grinding routine, we often imagine ourselves leaving winter behind and heading to Broome or Port Douglas or Darwin, probably with a fantastic-looking off-road camper trailer that will require a new LandCruiser to pull it. But have we shared that plan with our spouse? Have we asked them?

Yes? Well, good for you. Good luck. Go and do the Big Lap.

But if you haven't asked, you may be facing an uncomfortable reality, that while you are fantasising about landing a whiting on the beach at Hervey Bay, your partner might be thinking about what it will take to get a real-estate licence. Everyone says she has an incredible knack for engaging with people, and now that the kids have left home and an opportunity has presented itself, does she really want to forgo that freedom and spend months in a very confined space with you, eating too many dubious sausage rolls in outback roadhouses?

Maybe. Maybe not.

Don't assume.

Ask.

It was a sad reality for my mum that when my dad retired, he insisted that she did too. He wanted her company. She wanted to keep working. Mum loved the stimulation of work and the affirmation of being capable still. Why should she give that up?

But she did. Women did. All the time.

It's reality that a lot of long marriages come under pressure at this stage. You may both be padding around a family home that seems quiet and empty. Life might feel smaller. And without the distractions and obligations of a house full of teenagers, what you have left is what you started with.

Each other.

Now might be a very good time to reinvest in that person. And hold their hand. And not presume anything.

Australian Institute for Family Studies data shows the divorce rate among people aged in their fifties and sixties has climbed sharply in the past two decades. Nearly three in ten divorces these days involve couples who have been together for a long time. It is, as the *Forbes* writer noted, called grey divorce. And it's a bloody difficult time. More on that later.

Take a breath.

There's lots to think about, isn't there? There's plenty to worry about too, but there are also a few things to consider that might make your understanding of retirement very much easier.

This is important, I reckon.

When you go, go. Recognise it's over.

I resolved that when I left the media, I would try to park my ego and C-list celebrity status at the door. I don't quite know why I felt that mattered so much, but I did remember a sharp piece of advice I received many, many years before – indeed, just a few weeks after I arrived at ABC Radio Perth.

I'd settled in, begun to like the sound of my own voice, and perhaps sensing that, my producer pulled me aside with a big smile and said, 'When you leave this job, Geoff, people out there in radio land will be broken-hearted.'

I remember looking at Damian wide-eyed. I was already imagining how well liked I was to become.

'They'll be broken-hearted,' he repeated, 'for about three days. And then they'll have a new voice to listen to.'

You might imagine that the air roared out of my sagging balloon of self-belief, but it didn't. The point was well made. It was a great lesson.

When you leave, park your ego at the door. When you go, go.

I think we all know that, come Monday morning, you will not be quite the same person you were last Friday night at the pub, when your friends and colleagues said all those really nice things about you and that stunning young woman from accounts called you a silver fox. Come Monday, those same people will be sizing up whoever is now sitting in your office or leading the morning sales meeting. They will be keen to impress and win favour with someone. And it is no longer you.

And someone else, perhaps that young woman from accounts, might even say, 'It'll be a breath of fresh air to have someone else in charge.'

Professor Gary Martin puts it simply: 'Yeah, let's call it retirement realism. If you don't have an ounce of that, then you're going to struggle. You'll be grumpy. You've got to put yourself back in the shoes of an everyday person, someone who doesn't get preferential treatment.'

It seems a bit sharp-edged, doesn't it? This overnight loss of status.

Well, we've all heard a version of that joke that says the graveyard is full of the irreplaceable.

When the gig is over and the keys to the company car have been returned and your executive assistant is now attending to the diary of someone else, you no longer wield power or influence. And it might sting a bit.

Do you remember what Michael said about kind people telling him 'you will be snapped up'? Kind people and close friends and colleagues unsure what to say next are not the most reliable guides to the job market.

In the days leading up to my departure, people of reputation and influence spoke of lots of opportunities that would now come my way. Any number of board invitations or speaking engagements.

I'm glad I'm not waiting.

Surely I would be invited to deliver important speeches or lectures on the future of journalism – or on the role that media must play to ensure the future of our fragile democracies in these uncertain times? Surely.

While not wanting to chase further media opportunities – and very much wanting to concentrate on the creative challenge of writing this book – I did, however, imagine my inbox would still have a few invites for free grog and canapés. Hello? Anyone? How about a free film preview?

Crickets.

As I write this, I am laughing. I am grateful that I had no real expectations. And I was wise to not presume.

So I would urge you, perhaps those of you with a much broader CV of workplace expertise and achievement than me, to remain circumspect about what might open up for you now that you have the luxury of time. Opportunities may arise. Or they may not. The phone might ring. Or it might not.

You might keep checking if there are any messages, but there might not be any. If this happens, try not to take it personally. Use it as an opportunity to reboot and explore other things. But do know that you might have to find the energy and motivation yourself.

And please, please don't call up the office on Thursday afternoon and hope the person on the other end of the line has the time to engage in dreamy remembrance or the latest gossip. They are busy. You are not.

Gary Martin mentioned the importance of not just sitting in a chair watching the cricket or listening to the races all day. That advice was based on the experiences of his dad, a police officer who retired as a superintendent at the age of fifty-five. As Gary remembers it, his dad did travel a bit and tick a few things off his bucket list in the first couple of years, but after that he ran out of motivation and his life turned to stone.

'When we would go and visit, we'd find him in the same position all the time. In front of the TV in a recliner rocker,' Gary says. 'He had grandchildren, probably about ten at that time, who would come over to visit, and do you think he would move out of that chair? No one could interfere with that. When we came over, it was like, "Hi. Yeah, Mum's in the other room." My mum compensated for it to a certain extent. But he was so grumpy all the time that the grandkids were a bit scared of him. He retired too young.'

I'm guessing Gary's dad was from a similar era to my own father's. And like so many dads, he wouldn't budge or be helped.

Gary says even when his dad was diagnosed with cancer, he insisted his children not be told about it, because 'I don't want that to be part of their burden'.

'That's the sort of person we were dealing with. Still the hardened cop. Who decided that this is what retirement would look like.' He shakes his head with regret.

I know Gary has no intention of living his life the same way.

Have a pause.

Have a think.

Be confident you are going to have good discussions with the people you love about what it is you really want to get out of these next ten, twenty, maybe thirty years.

And allow yourself to have fun. Remind yourself of the things you loved to do as a kid – and go and do them again. I may yet hit a huge first serve that explodes off the chalk past a despairing racquet and whistles into the fence.

You have a renewed opportunity to go in pursuit of joy. How bloody great is that?

Chapter 4

Money

As we get older, more and more of us will be targeted with financial advice, crypto spam and invitations to 'click this link' for guaranteed happiness with a Nigerian prince. And we are particularly vulnerable, probably because so many us are absolutely terrified of running out of money in our retirement and dying penniless in the street.

I remember an old ad that showed a couple in their early sixties drinking tea and poring over the numbers.

She places her hand on his shoulder, looks worried and says something like, 'At this rate, we won't even be able to afford to retire.'

He looks admonished. He's failed as a provider.

The tagline says something like, 'If they'd invested with us, they wouldn't face the very real prospect of running out of money in retirement and dying penniless in the street.'

Then there are those superannuation ads where one neighbour is clearly far more financially literate than the other because he or she is part of an industry super fund rather than some other one. The implication from the smile of the first neighbour is that they are destined for a life of contentment, while the neighbour over the fence faces an uncertain future, filled with two-minute noodles and a kink in their garden hose.

Perhaps you've done your own research and sought the expertise available in any number of those lavish, usually American, get-rich-in-retirement books. They invariably wear titles like 'I Used to Serve Coffee and Now I Have My Own Servants' or 'How I Went from Bum to Billionaire in Three Years' and are written by people called Theodore J Peckinpah or Dr Sylvester Pickles III.

Be wary. The financial planning and advice industry has more than its share of gangsters, shysters, grifters and chancers.

That said, let me be very clear: your financial circumstances are entirely your business, and this book exists only to suggest a few tips to live a more contented and less cynical life. I am not going to give you financial advice.

It's entirely up to you if you want to buy shares in miracle fat-dissolving technologies or become a board member of a hopelessly underachieving non-league English football club. Indeed, if you want to send all your money to a beautiful young Belarusian woman who contacted you on Instagram and reckoned you looked really hot, then do it!

Do whatever you want to do. Invest in life as you wish to.

~

But I do have a friend who has been offering excellent general financial advice on ABC Radio for many years. His name is Nick Bruining, and he is a wise man of good intention. Consequently, I have asked Nick to reflect on a few things he knows to be true about you, me and money as we prepare for, or are living in, our retirement years. About the realities of our appetite for risk and reward. The fundamentals proven over time.

I'm going to the beach now, but will be back after Nick's little chat.

~

G'day, Geoff's readers,

Thank God he wears board shorts, that's all I say.

Hope the next paragraphs provide some clarity or ease a few worries and perhaps even help you make some good decisions.

This is a funny idea for a book, isn't it? But I suppose anything that makes us feel less inclined to be grumpy is a good thing. And money worries make all of us grumpy.

So let's begin with the obvious. As we lurch towards retirement, the question often arises: do I have enough money to last me through to the end?

It's a fair question, but clouded by variables that can have a big impact on the answer. And make no mistake, everyone's answer is different. First you need to work out: what's your end game?

Option 1 is to spend your last dollar on your last day. Not a great plan, because no one really knows when that will be. You will have to be spectacularly exact or damn lucky.

I like the idea that you peg out owing the bank several hundred thousand dollars.

Option 2 is to provide handsome amounts for your loved ones through an inheritance. The problem is, to maintain those sums, you might have to be willing to live a miserably thrifty retirement, spending as little as possible.

Think twice about that. Particularly if you think they're the kind of kids who'll blow the lot when they get their hands on it.

I prefer the idea that you help them now, when they need it. Not only will you have the opportunity to relieve them of some serious financial pressures, but you'll be able to experience the joy of seeing their faces light up when you tell them what you're going to do.

It's hard to see that joy when your face is covered with six feet of soil or you've been sprinkled over your 'favourite place' from a giant salt shaker.

Option 3 is to do what most people do. Have a bloody good time while you can, and the kids can have what's left. But let me tell you, that's easier said than done. If you've spent your life being careful, turning into an indulgent spendthrift will be difficult.

Here's the reality: many of us are reluctant to spend what we have built over the years. We often see that with the very old, who may have experienced deprivation and even food rationing in the wake of World War II. That same risk-averse attitude was passed on to their kids, now proudly wearing the badge of 'Boomer'.

Boomers hate debt and really hate getting ripped off.

So, if you've done it tough to get here, perhaps had a business that failed or endured years of high interest rates on your home loans, your attitude may well be: 'If it ain't on special, I'm not getting it.' You probably hate seeing any decline in your account balance, and when investment returns are down, you'll keep your hands firmly in your pockets. People with this mindset only feel comfortable being indulgent after they can see a profit. If the numbers aren't so good, they'll sit tight and might even head back to cheap mince and noodles.

Remarkably, the percentage of people in this group – people who die with a savings balance very close to their starting retirement balance – is extraordinarily high. Easily 80 per cent or more.

Incredible, isn't it? That so many of us have this determined default position.

Yet even if you don't start as a reluctant spender, time will change your attitude. This is important to realise.

In the first years of retirement, you'll relax the purse strings and do the things that you want to do and should be doing. Travel. Get the house tarted up. Buy your grandkids useless things that you always wanted for yourself.

But by the time you reach your late seventies? Bad news. You don't need any more Ryobi add-ons, crystal wine glasses or Swarovski Christmas trinkets and there's a good chance your two-week trek up the Amazon with an indigenous guide is behind you. You'll be spending most of your money on food, accommodation, energy, transport, medicine and ... that's about it. It's estimated that at this age we are spending 30 per cent less on expenses than when our retirement started.

The second, rather brutal reality is that if you're a couple, the probability of you becoming single rises every day.

No tips here on how you successfully nominate who gets to go first!

When it does happen, there'll be a further decline in household expenses. Probably another 25 per cent. This tells us that the required capital to fund your remaining few years is significantly less than what was required at the start.

The last piece of the puzzle is to have a basic understanding of one of the world's best retirement income systems – and arguably the most complicated.

The pension.

I reckon it's been designed as a joint conspiracy between public servants and financial advisers. It keeps the former fully occupied making changes and the latter fully occupied explaining them.

Here's some curious facts about retirement income arrangements in Australia. The less money you have for your retirement, the more money you'll get from the system. That's by way of pension payments. If you have too much money, you don't get anything. But if you have too much money and you spend that money on fun things, you will then start to get a pension, and the more you spend on fun things, the more pension you get. Of course, there's a limit to this approach, but there's also a sweet spot where you can effectively max out the system.

If we accept that the pension system is there to underpin at least some sense of financial security, then enjoying retirement should be our absolute focus. And with that approach to life, you won't need to watch Alan Kohler every night to see if the share markets have crashed.

~

Most of us – me, you and Geoff – hope to be relatively healthy and happy in retirement, and we simply want our money to do a couple of things: provide enough for us every fortnight to do what we *want* to do and provide enough when we *need* it.

The greatest barrier to achieving these things can be boiled down to one simple four-letter word: risk.

Retirement is not the time in life to be chasing double-digit returns. Double-digit returns only come with risk, but risk is a plaything for the young, who have time on their side. When you're twenty, five years for the share market to recover after a crash is like a nasty pimple on the chin. Slightly painful to start with, but it soon disappears over time.

When you're eighty and there's a major share-market crash? That could well be your tipping point into the next life. Upon which I cannot comment, because I have no idea what happens beyond the grave.

So with all these new insights, how should you approach retirement? I reckon this is a good rule of thumb: work with what you've got now.

Get a sense of what you want to do and how you'll pay for it.

Don't try to kill the pig by taking big risks in the last few years of work. There's a good chance it will end in tears because people who do speculate this way often end up as financial shark bait.

If you're dealing with less than $1.5 million in savings (not including the house), take the time to learn the basics of how the pension system works, because at some point in retirement, you'll almost certainly become eligible for a part pension.

Finally, this old financial planner has been to hundreds of funerals. It's a genuine privilege and honour being trusted with the innermost secrets of clients who, ultimately, I view as friends. I've sobbed like a baby with many widows and widowers, kids and grandkids.

No one I knew ever died having done everything they wanted to do. So, Geoff's readers, if you have the money and ability to do at least some of those things now, get on with it. We don't know when our time is up.

My simple and best advice? It's to borrow a slogan from, of all things, a shoemaker.

Retirement? Just Do It.

Chapter 5

Influencer Interlude

I hope you don't mind, but I'd like to check in on you. See how you're feeling. I'm curious to ask if the many thousands of words preceding these ones have indeed given you pause for thought. Have you been able to consider life with the prospect of a little less grump in it? And what it would feel like to relax those shoulders, just a bit?

Give it a try.

Maybe this morning you chose to ignore Mrs Drobny's Lhasa Apso and its anxious barking because you realised the poor little bugger just gets lonely when she goes to work. And as you sat behind another Camry driver who obviously didn't know where he was going, your instinct today was to back off the horn and give him a moment to get his bearings.

Isn't it a bit of a relief to know we don't always have to impose ourselves? Or have the last word?

~

Why don't we do a little grumpy reflex test? To see where we're at.

Instead of tapping your patella lightly with a hammer and observing how dramatically your lower leg bounces, how about I tap you on the bonce with the story of a YouTube sensation who, it seems to me, rather typifies the nature of fame in the early part of the 21st century. And perhaps, for some of you, the superficiality of the modern human experience.

How will you respond to him, I wonder. Will you recognise his talents as unusual or extraordinary? When you hear of the success he has enjoyed, will you acknowledge as remarkable his ability to monetise those talents? Or will you want to pull your eyes out? Or have him devoured by sharks?

Whatever your response, the fleeting nature of short-attention-span fame these days surely means that within a few months he may be forgotten. Supplanted by a cat that can play the banjo.

Ready?

So, back in 2017, a rather pasty-faced nineteen-year-old named Jimmy Donaldson, who calls himself MrBeast, made a YouTube video where he declared his intention to count to 100,000 nonstop on camera.

I know, you're shaking your head already. And don't ask me why he doesn't have a space in his name or why he considers himself a beast.

It's easy to find. I hit play.

'Screw it,' says MrBeast and then he starts: 'One, two, three, four ...'

This task, incredibly dreary as it is, will require great endurance. It will take nearly forty hours to complete. MrBeast will not leave his chair. I presume he wees into a bottle.

I'm interested enough to click ahead many hours.

'... 62,373, 62,374, 62,375 ...'

At this point, MrBeast is slurring his numbers, yawning and rubbing his right eye. The effort to keep his concentration must be exhausting; so too the nonstop naming of numbers, which are becoming an ever-bigger mouthful.

I head towards the end of this epic.

'... 97,233, 97,234, 97,235 ...'

As he gets closer to his target, he closes his eyes, rocks back and forward in his chair.

'... 99,999, 100,000!'

MrBeast leans back and reflects on it all. He concludes with, 'What am I doing with my life?'

He will later say he did it because he was bored.

Let's pause. What do you think of him so far?

Are you curious? Or is he an idiot?

Am I wasting your time even asking you to have an opinion of him? Would you prefer to watch someone explaining the engineering requirements of building a box girder bridge? Because that is real. That has purpose.

Well, let me tell you what came next.

In the seven years since young MrBeast made what appeared to be an amusingly gimmicky but essentially pointless video, it has been watched more than twenty-nine million times. And MrBeast has become a phenomenon. His YouTube channel is the most subscribed individual channel on the platform, with more than 233 million subscribers. He now has an estimated net worth of US$500 million. In 2023, *Time* magazine named him one of the world's Top 100 most influential people.

In what way does he influence?

Today MrBeast owns a fast-growing burger chain in the United States.

He sells chocolate bars and a seemingly endless range of merchandise. His videos and competitions, often with big money giveaways, draw huge online audiences. A couple of years ago, he recreated the *Squid Game* television series as a real-life event.

He has been suitably philanthropic. He spends money planting trees and removing plastic from the oceans and feeding the hungry kids of Africa.

And he's still keen on the weird stunt, including being buried alive in a coffin for fifty hours.

It's hard for me to get beyond thinking MrBeast is just a weird product of a weird world. An entertainment offering of his time, the way Harry Houdini or PT Barnum were in theirs. But he also understands keenly the phenomenon that is mass communication these days and how to engage and build a huge audience.

He once filmed himself giving a homeless man $10,000, and in response the money from ad revenue began to pour in. He told *Forbes* magazine, 'I don't want to play it up too much. It just felt good. It's a world where I take ten grand and light it on fire and make twenty grand.'

If that isn't a capitalist American wet dream, I don't know what is.

What's next? MrBeast doesn't rule out running for US president one day.

What do you think of him now?

~

Personally, I find it very hard to relate to anything he does, but that is probably generational. I wasn't brought up watching YouTube videos. And despite being a participant in the media for most of my life, I am suspicious of his motives and the public benefit. There is never enough public benefit.

But if you have kids or grandkids, there's a pretty good chance they know who MrBeast is. And for me, that's reason enough to be moderately engaged and at least familiar with his story. It's a bit like my mum and dad coming into the lounge room on a Sunday night to watch a few minutes of *Countdown*. They usually left saying 'What a bloody racket!' but later they might hum along when they heard the song again.

It's about engagement. Knowing what's going on with the kids.

As we get older, it is very easy to rely only on the familiar, the comforting, the certain. But I reckon a fascination with all things nostalgic, while wistful and fun sometimes, can also be a sign that we don't want to engage with the new. Those rose-coloured memories do nothing to encourage us to believe in the future.

Did the roast chook for the Sunday lunches of your youth really taste better than the roast chook of today? I don't think so. But it was a rare treat, so our anticipation was greater. And the memory invites us to return to our younger selves. That's why footy was better back then, and we could leave our front doors unlocked, and there was a real sense of community ...

You might insert etc., etc., etc. here, but I'm inclined to add blah, blah, blah.

We do need to keep stretching. We need to retain a sense of wonder about things we don't already know. Particularly when our grandkids want to talk to us about that man who counted to 100,000 'without stopping!'

I'll probably watch MrBeast's career progression with some interest, particularly if I am still alive to see him run for the presidency in 2044.

And to be honest, having made up that line about a cat playing a banjo, I'll probably go and check out whether such a thing really exists.

Stay curious. Even about those things you don't really care about.

~

(And I've just wasted thirty seconds of my life watching a 1978 Little Friskies cat-food ad from the United States that indeed features cats appearing to play banjos. But not very well.)

Chapter 6

The Harm Online

The heads of the world's biggest social-media companies, Meta, TikTok, X etc. are regularly brought before important government committees. There to defend their thrilling, deep-space, dark-web, mind-fuck technologies from allegations they're turning our children into zombies or school shooters or just really sad kids who won't eat their dinner or make eye contact.

Which they are.

Just recently, New York City mayor Eric Adams declared in a statement of the bleeding obvious that social media is a 'public health hazard' and an 'environmental toxin', saying young people must be protected from 'harm' online.

And that's why the nerds are called before senators and the Honourable This 'n That and asked whether they think it is appropriate for ten-year-old children to be able to access online chatrooms where people share a bizarre sexual infatuation with ... I dunno, let's come up with one ... how about office stationery?

'Certainly not,' the executives say, deeply wounded by any implication that suggests otherwise.

'Well, I'm glad we can agree on that.'

The gavel comes down and nothing ever happens.

~

We are told every day that smartphone addiction is the new pandemic, burning a toxic digital hole inside vulnerable, developing brains and making kids anxious and suicidal and really weird. And those of us who are a little older and haven't had to deal with this profound and perplexing challenge often like to declare: 'Where are the parents?'

Conveniently forgetting any of our own shortcomings in those roles, while curling our fingers into bombs of outrage as we state, yet again, how we remember when a phone really was a phone, sitting next to the teledex on a stand in the front hall, only to be answered by adults with posh, put-on voices: '931701 ... Hello, Hutchison residence.'

The thing is – adults have been complicit in the ruination of children forever.

For.

Ever.

Let's go back. For more than twenty years now, let's call it a generation, we've handed increasingly smart devices – the Nokia becomes the Apple – to our beautiful bubs in supermarket trolleys, GP waiting rooms and restaurant highchairs, all with the intention of keeping them occupied and distracted. Thus enabling us to trawl aisle five for environmentally friendly oven cleaners, or to compose ourselves ahead of that pap smear, or to just tuck into a huge plate of spaghetti, uninterrupted by their constant demands and smeary little hands.

And the kids are hooked. Because that world we have introduced them to is so bloody exciting.

We invented the bloody technology. We adults.

And before we had phones, we had television sets, and parents would shove the kids in front of the idiot box too. And it would babysit them while the adults snuck out for a quiet fag or, if a Disney film was on, a couple of drinks and a quick Chinese.

The current generation of parents are not ruining their children any more than I did mine or Mum and Dad did with me. So why do so many of us sneer and get so judgey and grumpy about all this? About today's version of the same thing: the freight train of technological change that is barging across our world at an extraordinary and seemingly unstoppable and immeasurable rate.

Is it because we believe we were different? Better somehow?

~

I've just had an incredibly warm memory.

Back when I was a kid, on every single day of the school holidays we'd burst out the back door and jump on our bikes, head into the bush and decide whether today we would build a new cubby or fight another war with the Germans or the Japanese. The cubbies were built on coastal sand and kept collapsing, which could get a bit boring, so we usually opted for a war.

We'd start with cap guns, and after you were isolated and shot dead, there was a mandatory ten-second count – 'Don't move!' Then it became more physical: there was hand-to-hand combat and we'd throw honky-nut grenades and occasionally get blown up by match-head-fuelled bolt bombs (which required deft handling).

We weren't good at deft handling.

And, of course, there was the unspoken rule that anyone who turned up and possessed anything of value – I mean anything – had to share it. Biscuits, lollies, chewing gum, jokes and exaggerated stories about older sisters, parents or that new spunk in the newsagent who I reckon would go off like a rocket. Not that any of us really knew what that meant.

Younger siblings, by definition, were the weakest and most complaining, which required them to be regularly tied up and taunted until they were all snot and tears and impotent rage. Older siblings, who invariably assumed all positions of authority, were more restless and impatient, the first to see new opportunity – an old car wreck or an abandoned shed or a freshly pinched copy of *Playboy* magazine.

And when it got late, and thoughts turned to hunger and home or the belting that might arrive should we not get there in time, we'd scramble enough money for a bottle of Fanta, which everyone shared and gobbed into before passing it on. And just as the sun was setting, we'd arrive with a slam of the screen door, sunburnt and exhausted and jubilant that we'd reached the dinner table before the third call.

Chops, peas, mashed potato and Peter's neapolitan ice cream to finish.

'What did you boys get up to today?' asked whichever adult could be bothered.

'Not much,' we shrugged.

Desperate to go out and do it again tomorrow.

~

Good story, isn't it?

But not much of it is true. It's a Tom Sawyer retelling. A story that gets told all the time of a childhood so much richer than any enjoyed today. True for some, of course, but often a clichéd counterfeit memory.

In actual fact, my school holidays were usually spent with the Stovell boys – playing cricket and watching endless television and thanking Mrs Stovell for the glass of Coke she'd just handed me. Treats I didn't usually get at home.

And then one day, one of the boys hooked up the absolute best thing. A new game from someone or something called Atari.

The game was Pong and we played it for hours, in a state of what today I might label hyper-arousal. It was a bit like tennis. You had to move a slider up and down to intercept a dot that was ricocheting across a centre line on the black-and-white screen at ridiculously sharp angles and hopefully send it back before the other player's slider could reach it. Frankly, it was fantastic.

Generationally, the Atari became the Commodore 64, which became the Nintendo Game Boy and the Sony PlayStation and the Xbox.

And that has always been my response to those of us filled with grumpy 'kids on their phones these days' bluster.

You know him. The bloke who struggles to relate to a kid seemingly in the thrall of that reflected light, fighting a war with technology far more advanced than a handful of honky nuts.

Know him? Maybe you are him.

Well, imagine if ten-year-old you suddenly had access to every game imaginable, all in this snug, warm, fits-in-your-hand device. It doesn't ask you to insert a twenty-cent bit to play it either. Imagine if you could use that device to be in contact, often anonymously, with incredible people anywhere in the world. The strangers you could meet, befriend, fall in love with, tease and even hurt. Imagine if you only had to type a word into a white space to be taken to places beautiful, terrifying and grotesque. And have your mind blown. Because it's interactive. Because it talks back. And asks if you would like to participate.

Who wouldn't be drawn to that? What kid wouldn't decide it was more interesting than a cubby or a war or that copy of *Playboy*?

Ten-year-old John Wayne would have loved it. Ten-year-old Clint Eastwood would have loved it. Ten-year-old Arnold Schwarzenegger would have loved it.

You would have loved it.

And so would your dad.

Thing is, it didn't fall into your lap when you were ten. It fell into theirs.

And we put it there.

And because adult hypocrisy is boundless, I'm delighted to say we are becoming just as addicted to its devilish charms. We adults are now abandoning our morning newspapers and our evening appointments with the six o'clock news to get more and more of our world view in the palm of our hand. Oh, and pictures of toddlers biting the ears of dogs on that fantastic Instagram page.

Don't believe me? Look in any airport lounge. See if you can find someone of your age to have a meaningful conversation with. You won't. They'll be playing online sudoku or furtively sneaking a look at a man having sex with a stapler.

And the social-media sites we are rightly so worried about? We're being drawn to them too. The kids have long abandoned Facebook because it's now filled with so many pictures of us, smiling with mouths full of bad teeth at a birthday party or a school reunion or that cruise down the bloody Danube. 'Oh look, here's a photo of Frank fixing his reticulation!' Our own community online. Who'd a thought?

And just the same way our kids and grandkids are finding friends and shared interests, we're discovering all those French Bulldogs or *Carry On* films or Buy, Sell and Swap sites.

A shared interest.

Many of us are members of a local community page. This is where we meet, when we don't go to town and sit on park benches and engage face to face anymore. This is where we meet to seek useful advice on which plumber will unblock the sink at the best price, or which cafe serves the hottest cappuccino. At its best, it's a great interactive asset. And yet, like any other site in cyberspace, it can be just as vulnerable to gossips, busybodies and even a kind of vigilantism – all of it empowered by the benefits of anonymity.

And, of course, it's home to OUTRAGE BINGO!

'What about the silent majority?'

'What is this country coming to?'

'I'm sick of minorities trying to run this country!'

'The whole thing has gone too far!'

'We're being managed by snowflakes!'

'They probably want another referendum and will blame the taxpayers again.'

Feel free to add your own. But try to be creative.

These are also the pages where people with too much time on their hands start posting about unusual characters walking down the street wearing hoodies and looking dubious. They implore everyone to 'stay safe' in some of the safest neighbourhoods imaginable. They warn us to 'lock up' because 'someone not from around here was seen around here' just yesterday.

It's not just our kids who get sucked into dangerously negative spaces. It's us.

~

So here's my tip for getting the best out of social media.

Don't hover over the comments section. Or buy into the conspiracy and anger and suspicion that underpins the comments. Politicians know not to. Sports stars are advised not to. You should know it as well. Otherwise, you'll be sucked into a vortex of harrumph that may initially seem oddly interesting or amusing, but soon engulfs readers in a pot of boiling negativity and anonymous judgement.

It is where people go to vent and, by extension, to target.

Let me give you a silly, random but completely legitimate example. I have just clicked on a modestly engaging article online that asks readers to nominate the Italian restaurants in their neighbourhood that make the best carbonara. An invitation, essentially, for us to write with delight about memories of pasta made from the golden yolks of Nonna's chooks and how we ate so much we almost fell into a carb coma.

Some readers engage with great goodwill and enthusiasm. And all of them are women.

'Remember,' chirps one, 'there's no place for cream in a real carbonara!'

'What's guanciale?' asks another. 'I see it in traditional Italian recipes all the time.'

And sure, as those female correspondents engage with goodwill and curiosity, bored, disinterested males seek to spoil the mood.

Richie observes that 'Italian is the most overrated cuisine'.

Clint, whose interest in this subject is surely modest, declares, 'I do not like pasta.'

Someone calling themselves The Voice adds, 'And pasta is only peasant food in Italy, so it's not that special, mate.'

One reader asks how many of these places make their own fresh pasta. 'None,' observes Mickey. As if he knows.

Lynne notes a new pasta shop near her and gives it the thumbs-up. James replies with, 'You'll get robbed before you even get inside.'

Every bloke who has chosen to engage with the subject has chosen to find fault. Every single one of them.

You may or may not agree with me. You might accuse me of going from zero to one hundred over a silly story about carbonara. Claim that I'm declaring it the thin end of the wedge of pecorino.

I don't think I am. It was such a casual sample. I'm just suggesting we shouldn't spend too much time in environments that seem to entrench contrariness and anger.

And beyond it being an expression of harrumph, does it achieve anything or change anything or make us feel better? And how much energy does it take? To be so belligerent. And kill someone else's enjoyment.

Don't read the comments. Better still, why not read the reviews of the restaurants again?

Maybe even gather up the family and declare that tonight we're going to Guido's, where the chef uses guanciale he sources from his brother's farm, and where the eggs really do come from Nonna's chooks.

And just before you drift into that carb coma, when you notice one of the kids staring at his phone, ask him what he's looking at. And when he shrugs his shoulders and says, 'Not much' – ask him if you can have a look anyway.

Chapter 7

Your Health

Q: Why do men die earlier than women?
A: Because they want to.

~

I remember the first time I heard that joke. I laughed and then I sagged. A statement of such dry defeat. Funny. Typical. Exaggerated, of course, but perhaps not by much.

The conclusion being that many men just get to a point where, with little scientific insight but a long history of being alive, we self-diagnose and declare ourselves 'buggered'. And if that's how it feels to us, what's the point going for a walk or having an alcohol-free day or even listening to that woman in an apricot Lorna Jane leotard explain the benefits of Pilates 'for the older male core'?

We know what's happening to us. Our stomach is getting fatter, our hair is getting thinner, we can snap a tooth eating a stale Mintie and we can only just make out the second line of letters on the eye chart. And then we just guess what's underneath. 'Is that a P or a B?' Inevitably, the results suggest we might be diabetes-vulnerable or glaucoma-suspicious or any number of earnestly delivered pathologised interpretations of what we already know.

We're 'buggered'.

So here we are, friends. A few pages about you and me and our health and our relationship with our GP and our general unwillingness to confront any of it.

And to help guide us gently towards a better health outlook, I've called upon a couple of highly experienced GPs to tell us what they see when blokes like you and me wander down the corridor and into their rooms. On the rare occasions we do. After a mate has just had a heart attack at fifty and it's scared the bejesus out of him and, if we're honest, us.

To convince these GPs to speak freely, I asked if they would prefer to use a nom de plume – the name of a doctor they admire. So let me introduce you to Dr Peter Venkman and Dr Leonard McCoy. The first you may remember as a Ghostbuster with PhDs in both parapsychology and psychology. The other, better known as Bones, the ship's doctor responsible for the health of the crew on the starship *Enterprise*. They are professionals of great expertise – if a bit nerdy.

When I talk to them, something is immediately apparent. They both know how much we men hate going to see our GP. So, for starters, they do want to reassure us. They'll be kind.

As Dr Venkman puts it, 'If we responded with, "Look, you fat bastard, you are literally moments away from a heart attack, a stroke, getting diabetes or being vulnerable to a range of cancers," you'd walk out the door and never come back.'

He's probably right, isn't he? So it's worth remembering they are on our side.

What, then, are they on the lookout for when fifty-plus-year-old us finally goes for a check-up?

Dr Venkman lays it out. 'We just want to open a dialogue with you but not overwhelm you. For guys in their fifties, the blood tests are a screening tool to see where you are at. To see early on how things are, or to assess the risk into the future. We look at your family history. And cover the basics. We check your blood count, liver function, kidney function, cholesterol, your sugar profile – and the prostate blood test as well. We want to spread the net reasonably wide to make sure we are not missing anything.

'Thing is, you might have felt bulletproof for years, and then, when the results come back, it can be quite a shock. I'm suddenly saying to someone I may have only just recently met that things in their lives must change. You might need medicine for a blood-pressure issue you're not even noticing or statins for a cholesterol problem you are not even feeling symptoms for.'

When I ask them why men seem so unwilling to go and see their GP, they answer in unison.

'Men are lazy and scared of being told they might have to change the way they live. Better not to know what might lie ahead.'

'Do you find that understandable or a bit pathetic?' I ask.

'Pathetic and understandable,' they agree.

They are men too.

Now, because this little book is intended as a guide to live better, less grumpy lives, and is not meant to be a fault-finding inventory, let me offer only a small piece of advice once you've been cajoled into making that overdue appointment for a check-up.

Don't lie to your doctor. You are merely repeating a pattern of deceptive behaviour they have seen many times before. How do I know? I've tried it too. It began with a simple question from my GP.

'You're a tall fella, Geoff, about six foot four in the old money, I'd guess. How much do you weigh?'

'About 115 kilos, I think.' I am already defensive.

His face betrays nothing other than interest in my answer. 'Okay, why not jump on the scales for me. It says, just under 120 kilos. A bit more than you thought?'

'That's funny,' I say, pretending to be surprised. I admonish myself for having so obviously lied to him. And so quickly.

I don't even consider backtracking. I must keep digging, and even hear myself suggest the discrepancy might be down to me wearing particularly sturdy boots today. I don't think he buys it.

'And how many drinks do you have in any given week, Geoff? How many units of alcohol?'

'Hmm.' I ponder this as if I am really trying to do the sums. I am doing no such thing. I furrow my brow and then offer another strangled and unconvincing reply. 'About average, I would guess.'

We both know this is not true, but apparently it can't be easily proven, unlike the question of my weight.

Dr Venkman pitches in here: 'The trouble is, the liver is such a forgiving organ right up until the bitter end. Blokes must be drinking a lot of alcohol for a long period of time for it to show up there. So we take you on trust. Initially.'

I then self-justify by banging on about having several alcohol-free days during the week and only really having a drink on the weekend. I do not tell him that I am having a lot of drinks on the weekend. I do not tell him that when I tip the bottles into the recycling bin on Sunday night, the sound reverberates around my quiet suburban street like a horrendous cacophony of shame.

Dr McCoy: 'Most of us drink more than we ever admit. Socially, we drink a lot, and if we do it in a sustained way, it will damage us, just as it damages society more broadly. I have some people who come in and it's almost like a confession. Their alcohol use is an expression of something else going on in their lives. Which means I have to gently ask them if they are using it as a coping mechanism. And that can be more revealing. I see a lot, a lot … of closet, clandestine drinkers.'

At this point, I'd like to introduce a friend of mine, Pete the Plumber – he's not a closet, clandestine drinker; he just reckons that a trip to his GP might have saved his life.

A married father of two, Pete's been a long-time smoker and, yes, a thirsty drinker and has spent most of his working life up to his armpits in other people's squelchy ablutions. He has built a big, successful business, but it has come at some cost.

'Geoff, I'm fifty-six years old and I've been a maintenance plumber for just over thirty years. About eighteen years ago, I fell off a roof and managed to break my left ankle and fracture my right heel. It was that typical scenario where I was rushing to get through the day's workload, and I made a critical mistake. I went flying and landed on both feet from about three metres up. It's not the fall that did the damage; it was the landing.

'Once I had the surgery on the ankle and heel, my health deteriorated. Constant exhaustion and extreme pain in both feet and a general malaise had me looking for answers. After nearly two years and many blood tests and scans, I was referred to a rheumatologist, who diagnosed me with psoriatic arthritis.

'Earlier this year, things became a bit of a struggle. Climbing a small hill was beginning to feel like a mountain. So I decided to go to my GP for all the old-man checks (diabetes, cholesterol, liver, kidney function, heart etc.). Surprisingly, all the results came back fine. Given my family's history of diabetes, I was astounded! My GP did ask me to go for a heart scan, as my cholesterol reading was slightly high, and given I was a long-time smoker, there was a matrix that could possibly correlate with heart disease.

'After having the CT dye scan of my heart, it was revealed I had a very badly blocked main artery. A week or two later, I had a stent inserted. They said the old artery was 95 per cent blocked. I was this far away from having a heart attack or a stroke. Mate, I didn't realise heart disease is the biggest cause of death in men over fifty.'

Pete had always justified his smoking by saying he would give up the gaspers as soon as he had a sign they were doing him harm. Now he had no choice.

'Six weeks after the stent went in, I started cardio rehabilitation, which included a six-week course of mixed cardio and strength workouts, and education on lifestyle, diet and ways to avoid heart disease. Since the cardio rehab, I've tried to turn my life around, and I hit the gym for an hour or so at least two or three times a week. I've cut back on the booze and stopped smoking altogether. I feel great. Exercise is one of the best drugs I've ever taken.'

Now you may think Pete's story is just something I plucked from a Heart Foundation pamphlet, but he's real. And now he reckons every day is a bit of a bonus.

The great challenge, of course, was to admit that he was struggling. Pete went to his GP and had all the tests. And he is living proof of their value.

~

So let's consider the experience of going to the GP.

How often do you go?

It would be great if you said, 'Regular as clockwork. Every twelve months, just to have my bloods done and a check-up.'

But I sense that is not the norm. We usually go to the GP only when something feels very wrong and we can no longer ignore it. As Pete did.

Whatever reservations you have about becoming a fitter, healthier you, you share that scepticism with most Australian men. You, me and just about everyone else is fearful about going to the GP and being told there might be something wrong. Because that inevitably leads to conversations about whether we are prepared to confront some of our poorer 'choices' and consider making 'lifestyle' changes.

One suggestion might be to ease off those petrol-station sausage rolls or perhaps have a read of this pamphlet about gut health – but that's not how we hear it. We hear it as an order to cut out pretty much everything we enjoy in life. First, they came for the Chiko Rolls ...

I ask our GPs what aspect of our behaviour they would most like us to change.

Dr McCoy jumps in: 'Lifestyle changes are important and they are worth it. And sometimes those changes will be hard. We all like drinking wine and smoking, and it's easy to not want to exercise much, but we have to go and do all the boring stuff. And yes, that means eating less fat, eating less chocolate, eating fewer biscuits.'

Dr Venkman: 'I really think for most patients, regular exercise is what I would most recommend. It helps with chronic pain, the joints, the cardiovascular concerns, and it's good for our mental health. If I had a superpower, it would be to get all my patients to exercise more regularly.'

When I ask our GPs how many of us, in a random sample of ten, will commit to cutting down on the grog, eating better food and taking more exercise, they think for a moment and can produce a score of no higher than four.

Out of ten.

They then settle on three.

And both stare off into the distance, wondering perhaps if they shouldn't have specialised in the tummy-tuck and lip-plumping business, rather than trying to keep blokes well.

The curious thing about all this is that the evidence is irrefutable.

~

What do the statistics tell us?

Here's the Australian Institute of Health and Welfare on 'The Health of Australia's Males' (27 June 2023):

'Australian males experience different health outcomes to females. Leading causes of ill health and death for males include suicide and self-inflicted injuries, coronary heart disease and dementia.

'Males are more likely to engage in risky health behaviours such as tobacco, alcohol and other substance use, physical inactivity and poor dietary choices. More males than females are overweight or obese. Males are also less likely to seek health care such as general practitioners (GP) and health professionals for their mental health.'

It's stark, isn't it?

What it strongly suggests is that we men are often going about our day-to-day lives feeling a bit off colour or a bit anxious and maybe a bit lost. The fact is that male suicides make up three-quarters of all suicides in Australia. And we aren't much good at asking for help.

So, we are eating and drinking and smoking too much and not getting good exercise. And the foods we like to eat most are engineered to tantalise our tastebuds with sweetness and salt and fat. And we can't get enough of it.

IBISWorld research from 2023 revealed that fast-food revenues in Australia had for the first time surpassed $23 billion. And stacked on top of the beers and the wine and the Scotch ... And stacked on top of the smokes ... The inevitable consequence over time is that things begin to groan and creak and spill and leak. And we get flabby and fat. And our muscles waste and our strength ebbs. And we can't be bothered to get off the couch. And our cocks become soft and strangely unfamiliar, no longer the missile system we have trusted and indeed held onto with such reliance for most of our lives.

(Just letting you know, if that last observation seems confronting and distasteful, there's more to come in Chapter 12, which is about our sexual health.)

And yet the report on 'The Health of Australia's Males' also tells us something that, frankly, makes me want to go and shake each and every one of you firmly by the hand. The report also tells us that nearly 60 per cent of us rate our health as excellent or very good. You beauty!

Deluded? Perhaps. A bit.

Despite evidence that says one in two of us are living with some kind of chronic condition. Or that in the next year nearly 100,000 of us will be diagnosed with some form of cancer. Or that nearly one in two of us will have a mental-health problem at some time in our lives.

How do we respond? 'Nah, mate, I'm good. Fit as a fiddle. And sound as a bell.'

~

Dr McCoy admits that patients who continue to smoke cause him the greatest frustration.

'Smoking I'm a lot more didactic about than alcohol use. Its impacts are quicker and more damaging. You are more at risk from all types of cancers if you continue to smoke, and there are no redeeming features. The science and the messaging are pretty simple. If you stop smoking, your blood pressure comes down, your risk of heart attack comes down, and I tell patients if they can manage that, they will have done more in that single act than I will ever be able to do for them.'

Clearly, to be a fitter and more active and happier version of ourselves, we can't ignore those 'lifestyle' choices. If we are drinking too much, smoking, eating an unbalanced diet and not getting enough exercise, our big loving selves are vulnerable to just about every awful illness and ghastly death you can think of.

A life that might suddenly be cut short. Or a life dogged for years by illness and pain.

This is personal stuff, and lectures don't work. We must reach our own conclusions.

As I consider all this, hoping I haven't been too preachy, I am staring at a bowel-cancer prevention kit that has just arrived in the mail. And for a moment, I sigh.

And then I laugh.

Think what you will of government, but every few years it cares enough to say, 'We don't want Australians to die of bowel cancer. I wonder if Geoff has had his poo tested lately?'

~

The last word belongs to my mate Pete the Plumber. Part of his motivation to try to live a better life comes from the memory of his dad, who in retirement after years running a servo rather lost his way.

'Dad retired abruptly, and when he did, he didn't have any hobbies or pastimes apart from being down at the bowling club. By that time, he'd become the archetypal grumpy old man and was feared by all the grandkids, and to be honest, other people didn't want to be around him too much.

'Dad died last year, and I've been reflecting on his life and the things that would have made him happier as he aged. Having a wider group of friends and acquaintances, taking care of your health and having hobbies and interests are, I think, pretty critical.

'Thanks, Dad, for giving me the insight to be happier.'

Chapter 8

Take a Look in the Mirror

What do you see when you look in the mirror, first thing in the morning?

Oh no, is he really going to ask this?

Yes, dear reader, I am.

Do you interrogate the face staring back at you or just seek confirmation that it's still there? I lean towards the latter. I'm not sure blokes of my generation have spent a lot of time considering what we see in the bathroom mirror. For many of us, it suggests a vanity or finicky self-indulgence that was never to be encouraged.

A legacy perhaps of teenage years in the small, shared family bathroom. A safe place, we thought, where poses were practised, penises measured, pimples exploded and hair gel applied to shape a different version of ourselves, only for a sibling to burst in, shouting with humiliating glee, 'Errr, love yerself, why don't ya? You look like a dickhead.'

Or a parent. 'Now put that back. It's your sister's. We'll say no more about it.'

And so, it was just more practical as we got older to join the ranks of the shit, shower and shave crew, before easing into the wear-every-day uniform of male conformity and convenience. More practical to just get on with it. Whatever it was.

On reflection? Well, it did dovetail nicely with the unspoken ethos of the times, I suppose: don't be too pleased with yourself or talk about 'feelings' or present an aspect of yourself that is anything other than completely conventional. Extraordinarily efficient, really, how we somehow managed to box up all that male complexity and nuance and belittle any attempt to explore it as complacent self-absorption – or wanting to look like Boy George.

'You weirdo. I'm telling Mum.'

Sure, it probably did stunt our emotional development and harm our mental health, but there was one valuable upside that needs to be acknowledged. It also meant we could be relied upon in times of crisis to jump into the shower and pledge with absolute commitment, 'I'll be ready to go in five minutes!'

By spending as little time as possible looking in the mirror, we became very punctual. And reliable. That tremendous trait of us blokes.

Reliable.

Now. Fancy taking this book into the bathroom, closing the door and having a bit of a stare?

Yes, try to get beyond the fact that it sounds a bit weird. I'm not asking you to go live on GrumpyPorn, where naked men of a certain age leer at the camera and express their frustration with local government authorities. Of course not.

Just go and have a look. Give yourself a full five minutes to just stare at the face you offer the world every day.

What is it you notice first?

The George Clooney resemblance? The family dog resemblance? Someone familiar and friendly? Someone you and others like?

That'd be good.

How quickly, though, do you go looking for fault? With the intention of what? Remedying it? Fighting the flab? Beating the bulge? Straightening the shoulders and lifting your chin? Or confirming your worst suspicions that today you are indeed a day older than yesterday and that means you'll die sooner?

So many questions. Here's another. What is it you recognise first?

Puffiness around the eyes? A mouth dragged by gravity into an unintentional and seemingly permanent frown? An exploded airbag where your chiselled jaw used to be? Guts that you can only suck in for a moment before they succumb to an irresistible, cascading lava flow? Creepy, crepey skin on your arms? Blotches, wrinkles and the stalks of skin tags that appear to have grown overnight on your neck? Hair sprouting from your ears? The ever-present need to de-forest?

The loss of something you once had?

The person you once were?

Who isn't coming back?

Okay, based on that, look away now. I understand why we can't get away from that mirror soon enough. We don't want reminding that decrepitude is coming or that we'll soon be giving off a smell of boiled cabbage or musty books.

The Japanese even have a word for old-person smell. They call it *kareishuu*. And from what I understand, it's not meant unkindly, nor is it unpleasant. The term or the smell.

So there's that.

My turn. Stop hogging the mirror. 'Errr, love yerself, why don't ya!'

~

What do I see?

I see a big man with a big head, and the weight of being me will become increasingly burdensome as I get progressively rounder and more stooped. A friend of mine who is even taller once declared with scientific and fatalistic certainty that the future will not be kind to us, the larger dinosaurs. We will fall over and not be able to get up.

I've got a few minutes left ...

There is a sagging right eyelid, the result of a weird encounter with Bell's palsy as a teenager. It causes weakness in facial muscles, so when I get tired, it droops. So too the right side of my mouth, which when I'm sleeping makes me look enfeebled and prone to dribbling.

I wish my hair was still black, but all those years in talkback radio turned it grey and then white.

My face now looks increasingly vague. Nondescript.

And yes, I am growing skin tags on my neck.

On the upside, there is a twinkle in my eyes. I grin easily. And I know it reflects me as I am. As I was in my Year Ten school photo. Someone who loves to laugh. Someone who is glad to be here still.

Sometimes, though, I wonder what sanctimoniousness looks like and if this small smile is too self-satisfied. Too bloody pleased with itself.

I hope my five minutes is up.

Even if the look in the mirror is a cursory one, we need to like what we see, well enough at least to give ourselves a pass mark and entry into each day. And to give ourselves permission and opportunity to explore life a bit more and maybe even find something pleasurable. Opportunity to fight back against gravity, which makes us look grumpy even when we are not.

If you're still in the bathroom, return to the mirror and produce a big grin.

It looks alright, doesn't it? Admittedly a bit horror-film garish if you hold it too long, but a version of it is worth offering up, now and then. It makes you look so much younger. Like George Clooney or a handsome schnauzer.

~

Back in my earlier Daggy Dad days, I would occasionally ask our two little kids – as they were cleaning their teeth before bedtime in one of our two bathrooms – what they saw when they looked in the mirror.

They would shrug. Unable perhaps or unwilling to describe themselves for a big lump of a man asking a dumb question that was impinging on their time with Stephen Fry reading *Harry Potter and the Philosopher's Stone*.

I'd follow up with, 'Do you like what you see?'

They'd usually grin and say yes. They knew this by rote.

And then a third question. 'Do you have a good heart?'

'Yes,' they'd say, nodding their heads furiously, perhaps drawing more on reflex than accumulated life experience.

I guess I wanted them to know the question was important enough to consider when any of us look in the mirror. That the better, more contented self is something worth aspiring to.

It was important for me as their father.

And yes, I was after an affirmation that they were happy and that I could be confident they would grow into adults with good, kind hearts.

And they have.

Pause.

Even longer pause.

And I've just realised, for the first time, why I might have asked this of them and whether it indeed had echoes of the same question I asked on a hot February afternoon about forty years earlier.

'Are you happy, Dad?'

And yes, it might have something to do with the old man. And a seemingly unfulfilled life. And my desire for something better. And more at ease.

Before we move on, I need you to know that this tendency I have towards homily-filled sentimentality, which even I find irksome when I dial up my cynicism meter, is not really my fault. I blame Will Robinson from *Lost in Space*. If there was a childhood role model who meant the world to me, it was Will. For a kid only a year or two older, he was smart and practical and a quick learner. He was empathetic. He formed a friendship with a robot, and the pair of them talked about their feelings, even though robots weren't meant to have them.

I can still hum the sad incidental music from *Lost in Space*.

'Der, der, der, der, der ...

... der, der, der, der ...'

Isn't it great?

Will was sensitive and supportive and caring, even of Dr Zachary Smith, a manipulative monster who regularly put the Robinson family at incredible risk and who these days would probably be on a paedophile watchlist. Will saw the best in everyone. There was no challenge or responsibility for which he would not volunteer.

If I was to sit down and watch an old episode today, I reckon I would still admire that nerdy, naive do-gooder. And even catch a glimpse of him in the mirror.

Go on. Take another look.

I hope you like what you see, well enough to offer yourself up to the world again today.

And do that grin again. It's hilarious.

Okay, stop now.

Chapter 9

Why We Have to Work at Friendships

Do you get together with mates? How often?

Do you have mates? Or is there another chapter to write, called 'Might there be a reason why I don't have any mates?' We'll set that aside for now, but the answer might be that you probably don't invest in them anymore.

You may be fond of old schoolfriends or work colleagues, but when was the last time you called them for a yarn?

I have a very dear friend who lives many thousands of kilometres away, having forged a stunning media career in the United States. When I ring him, we are immediately transported to other times and shared experiences. We are again younger, more handsome and completely hilarious versions of ourselves. Later in the conversation, relaxed and very much at ease, we talk about our kids, reflect on our careers, the onset of arthritis and how we think the next years might pan out.

I enjoy it immensely, and the conversation always ends with him determinedly declaring, 'We have to do this more often.'

Why We Have to Work at Friendships

He never rings. I do.

He tells me that today he has very few friends. In fact, he's a self-proclaimed loner. And he's happy enough with that.

He's a lovely bloke. He just doesn't try very hard.

If he tried a little bit? Well, I guess that's his business. And I don't care. Perhaps in my earlier days I might have wondered why I was making all the effort, but these days it seems such an easy conversation for me to start.

If a friendship is to be more than a shared history, if it is going to remain meaningful, then it has to be nurtured. And I know that word has some of you grinding your teeth, but it's true. Even our mates need a little love.

A nurtured friendship is not just about a comfortable nostalgia, it's about the potential of what comes next. What will the next stage of our lives look like? How far away is that finish line?

Will I stay well and happy? Will I, as statistics dictate, be spending some of those years in poor and declining health? Will I be able to live at home? And what if the person I love most dies before me? Will I lose my marbles and bark every time the bus goes past? What will I do then? How will I cope? Will I be okay?

Admittedly, it's not very aspirational. There's not a lot of high-fiving going on. I don't see a lot of us blokes linking arms and marching towards our destiny accompanied by 'The Final Countdown'. But it's also fascinating. And bloody interesting. There's still a lot to talk about.

I want mates to help me to find clarity and context and, yes, to retain a sense of wonder about the great unknown and that ever-shortening road ahead. And I want us all to be surprised at our ability to be occasionally delighted and often very funny company. And I want to be there when they need me.

Who doesn't like the idea of that?

Just a warning, though, if you are easily triggered by the word 'nurture': it appears again later in this chapter.

In the meantime, if you don't feel quite like offering a warm hug to everyone you've ever met, I have a great tip to get you started. Particularly if words don't always come easily to you.

Send a text.

Say anything. Say 'G'day' or 'Hope you're having a good day'.

Take a moment to tell someone you like that you're thinking of them. Do it with your kids or grandkids.

Invest a little and be rewarded for it.

Even if your text is just to express the view that 'This book your mother bought me is really starting to give me the shits. Hope the interview goes well.'

Just engage.

And if they respond, engage again.

But then let them go, because they probably have a busier life than yours.

What is there to lose? Nothing but your indifference.

~

I do wonder sometimes whether in Australia we have set the bar of mateship impossibly high. We mythologise it.

When I think of mateship, I think of those beer ads with sweat-soaked Aussie blokes – who've been shearing sheep or fighting wars or inventing

Wi-Fi – turning up to the pub in their blue singlets and downing a cold one. The Victoria Bitter soundtrack, which has inspired Australian patriotic fervour for more than half a century, swirls in the background as those men mime their tall tales and throw their heads back and roar with collective white-toothed laughter or a more reflective nod and a wink.

'Good on yer,' they seem to be saying. 'You bloody beauty.'

Mates understanding the world and each other.

It used to be beer. Now it's gambling ads.

And even though mateship is a rather bastardised concept these days – diminished by advertising agency clichés and by politicians desperate for you to accept them as a beer-drinking Digger – the idea itself is based on something deeply and intrinsically important to us: connection. Other versions of you and me. Opportunities to befriend and share and rely upon. A sounding-board. A mirror.

And perhaps, if you're willing to explore it, an antidote to loneliness and ever-growing cynicism about the state of the world.

And even though you may be at an age where, like my old friend, you think you can't be bothered to meet new ones, you should try. They're out there. Ready and waiting for your friendship too.

Be it at the pub. A men's shed. A food-bank production line always desperate for volunteers. A book club. A footy club. A men-only craft-beer and belly-dancing class. It doesn't matter.

The fact is, we need to be with other men. We need to share the space. We need to share ourselves to see ourselves.

And I wonder how good at that you are?

Pause. We both look around. I'll take the shoulder shrug and deep sigh as the answer 'Pretty average, I suppose.'

I wonder too what you and your male friends talk about.

A 'once-over lightly' temperature check of family and health and happiness?

'How's Fiona?' 'Good.'

'How are the kids?' 'Good.'

'Is young Brandon out of jail?' 'Yeah, I think so.'

'And how are you travelling?' 'Can't complain.'

Or are you more likely to discuss with forensic focus the footy draft?

I can see you leaning in. I can hear the burble of banter as you excitedly tell me, if we trade that kid to Sydney as part of a three-way deal, probably with Port Adelaide and Hawthorn, it should free up some salary-cap space for us to swoop on that fantastic young bloke from country Victoria who all the pundits reckon has a really good set of hands for a player of his size.

Whaddya reckon? Nothing wrong with that either. (We'll be talking more sport later.)

On reflection, that first conversation, the temperature check, might, in about an hour from now, prise open something really important or scary or wonderful if we are prepared to commit to it.

The second conversation flows more easily and asks and risks little. Accepting that generalisations abound here, most of us tend to opt for the second conversation. Less hassle.

It's often argued that women socialise 'face to face' and men 'shoulder to shoulder'. The suggestion is that we are better communicators when we are doing things together, performing a task. Shearing sheep, fighting wars, inventing Wi-Fi. Friendship based on shared experiences and perhaps shared silences.

Professor Gary Martin, who we met earlier, has written extensively on the 'bromance drought'.

I know. You probably don't like that phrase.

He says, 'There are any number of plausible explanations for the current middle-aged male friendship recession. One theory is that men have increasingly become time poor, to the point that social activities with mates have become their lowest priority. Work, parenting demands and even caring for older parents make it near impossible for men to invest the time needed to establish good and lasting friendships.'

I wonder if that's your experience. I do remember being in the thick of teenage-years parenting, and with both of us working, it was rare to find more than an hour or so for a quick beer and a catch-up with mates. As much as I enjoyed their company, we could never find the time to build something more meaningful.

And yet I probably didn't need that. I just wanted a laugh and a beer and male company.

But the prospect of building a substantive relationship? Unlikely. There were so many other things that needed to be done.

Gary – who I reckon I could very easily become a mate with, because he laughs at pretty much all my jokes and, as a result, makes me feel good about myself – offers some useful advice.

Essentially, he says, we men have to invest if we want real friendships. Everything else is just banter. Frothy beer and bullshit down the pub.

He reckons there's even a formula.

'Geoff, some experts have added substance to the argument by pointing out that friendship responds to the formula 11–3–6. In other words, to convert an acquaintance into a true friend, there needs to be a minimum of eleven meet-ups, with each clocking in at three hours or more, across a half-year span.'

Gary knows you don't much care for formulas.

'Perhaps the most important way to climb out of the current drought is to acknowledge that friendships – either those from one's younger years or ones formed in later life – will only remain viable if they are regularly nurtured.'

Did you notice he used the word 'nurtured' too? I did warn you.

Look, we can sometimes be intimidated or suspicious of new words and phrases because we don't understand their intent. And we aren't all comfortable pondering the 'authentic us' or our 'inner voices', but really ...

Nurture your friendships.

Go on. Send that text.

I know I'm badgering you a bit. But Gary's conclusion is obvious: 'Like so many things in life, men's friendships represent yet another case of *use it or lose it*.'

~

I caught up with an old schoolfriend recently, who, when I asked if he risked becoming a bit grumpy, declared defensively and a bit grumpily, 'Not really.' After all, he regularly gets together with some mates for a coffee on a Saturday morning.

'What do you talk about?' I asked.

He laughed. 'Oh, you know, how you're not allowed to say anything anymore these days!'

His coffee mornings apparently involve compiling lists of the latest outrages connected to a woke world and the conspiracy of cancel culture.

Probably including Benny Hill falling out of favour.

'Are blokes really not allowed to say anything anymore?' I asked with sly intent. 'Or are we just encouraged not to be domineering dickheads?'

'Bit of both,' he conceded.

That's something.

This group comes together because it has a shared view of the world and finds comfort in the reassurance of that position. Fair enough. We like the validation of others. That group of friends is still very important. But that friendship group might also be a silo of sameness, and we have to ask ourselves whether that can be self-defeating. Whether it lacks curiosity. Or much hope.

My friend replies that his group exists, in part, as a response to changing times and polarising issues. He cites the politics of gender as an example. 'What about Gen Z or whoever they are and their trans agenda? I'm sick of being told how ignorant and disrespectful I am for mixing up they/them pronouns!'

I don't want to tell my friend I think he is being sucked into a contrived fight that seeks to vilify the vulnerable and different. That would be boring of me. And, to his ears, probably both pretentious and self-righteous. Nevertheless, we need to be wary of silos. They do not invite understanding. They do not value differing opinions. And we are not being well served because of them.

I hope you agree. You might not.

~

There is and always has been conflict between old ways and the new. I was reading a piece in *The New York Times* by Brad Stulberg, who writes about men's mental-health issues. He notes that many people try to deny or resist or control change, but argues it doesn't have to be that way.

'Like it or not, life is change. We'd be wise to shift our default position from futile resistance to being in conversation with change instead.'

Pretty simple, huh? We can rail against change or we can find the curiosity within to want to understand it better. We don't have to like it very much, but we can remain engaged or we can choose to let it pass without taking the requisite offence or feeling that indigestion burn in our guts. And in an increasingly polarised, tribal world, we would surely benefit from that.

(I look forward to you meeting Gemma later on.)

~

The other day, I was invited by a fellow dog owner to join him and some other local blokes who have started an informal group that meets every month. With a couple of exceptions, they were strangers to one another. But they were drawn by a willingness to meet new people and hear what they might have to say. About anything.

Interestingly, they agreed not to meet at the pub, because that would carry with it the implication and the temptation and the pressure to just drink together. Instead, they gather around a long table at a pizza joint and bring snacks and a couple of bottles of red. And they just talk.

I went along. I sat between a bloke named Tom and another bloke named Tom, and what I noticed immediately was how they all leant into the conversations swirling around them. Now, that might be because we are all getting a little deaf, but the body language was really positive and eye contact mattered.

What did they talk about? Everything. But they listened hard too. Glad to hear stories and opinions they hadn't heard a hundred times before. Glad to have found new voices.

And the group is growing. Don't call it a Men's Anything. It's just a loose collection of blokes building a connection.

And they'll be there next month. Expecting nothing much from each other, but willing to offer something of themselves.

The fact is, engaged, curious men make friends more easily and are less likely to be vulnerable to the myriad of health concerns that gnaw away at us as we age. Engaged, curious men are less likely to be grumpy and lonely. Engaged, curious men have lots of people who care about them. And like them.

~

Have a little read of the following. It's a kind of manifesto from another place where men gather, called the Good Blokes Company.

'Hidden beneath a thin facade of stoicism lies a silent plea for change. Our culture of masculinity has become a labyrinth of expectations that trap and suffocate the souls of men and boys. In the relentless pursuit to prove ourselves as man enough, we have forgotten that strength is not found in the absence of emotion, but in the courage to own it. As male suicide rates soar and violence shatters lives, men across Australia are coming to terms with the fact that this is our problem to solve. It is up to us to redefine what a "good bloke" is. To take responsibility for our emotional lives and to hold each other accountable to a better way of being.'

What do you think of that? It's powerful and poetic in its own way.

And you might dismiss it as a bit New Age Hippy Dippy. That's up to you. But to me it is a passionate, insightful call to arms. A plea for blokes to start talking about things that matter.

Their emotional wellbeing. Their feelings. Your feelings.

Now before you shout out, 'That's it, I'm off!'

Stick around.

That 'thin facade of stoicism' is probably you and me saying 'I'm alright' not because we are, but because we don't want to reveal that we might not be. Trapped and suffocated souls? If you grew up in a household where Dad did not express his fears or concerns, then what's the likelihood that you were encouraged to do the same? Not much. This is the legacy we blokes have to address, according to the man behind the Good Blokes Company, Mike Dyson.

I ask Mike to cast his eye over his words so we might better understand them.

'As I read this again,' he says, 'the bit that jumps out at me is a "silent plea for change", and I think there are a lot of us who have been taught not to express our emotions, to not talk about our emotions, to not ask for help and even to not deeply look within.'

Mike is in his forties, the son of a Vietnam vet, a father of three daughters. He's very friendly. Completely engaged with the subject. When I ask him why it matters so much, his eyes moisten and his voice catches.

'I get emotional as soon as people ask me that. Because people are dying, Geoff. Eighty-six men in Australia call an ambulance every day because they are worried about suicide. I'm a father of daughters and an uncle of nieces and nephews, and I think there are a lot of people out there not getting the support they need. So they are hurting themselves and hurting others.'

As I look across at Mike, I see someone generationally braver than me. I see a new version of an old model. Open and honest. Vulnerable but accountable. It could be a good model.

Mike runs seminars on what it is to be a good bloke these days. He talks to corporate CEOs and men who run footy clubs. He talks with schoolteachers about the boys in their classes. And yes, he has also run dads-and-sons rites-of-passage camps. And even before you ask, he responds, laughing: 'We don't sit around singing "Kumbaya".'

'Mateship is something we talk about a lot in this country,' he says, 'but do we have supportive mateship? Do we have accountable mateship?'

I'm not sure Mike isn't an afficionado of 'Kumbaya', so I decide to go along to one of his seminars to investigate further.

~

The seminar marks the start of Movember, the men's mental health awareness month, and today Mike is addressing employees of the Water Corporation. He's also nursing two broken ribs, which he admits has been a bit hard to deal with of late. 'Pain,' he says with great curiosity, 'has a way of impacting everything you do. It's fascinating.'

Mike finds having broken ribs fascinating. He's an unusual dude.

He's here to tell the audience of the dangers of Lone Wolf Syndrome – what happens to men when we retreat from the world and each other.

'If I'm a guy who doesn't ask for help, is not trusting of others, or relying on others, or risking the vulnerability of deepening a relationship with others, is it any surprise that by the time I reach my thirties, I might now be the father of a six-month-old baby and feel that no one has my back? Do I ever allow others to know that I have stuff going on? Do others know I'm struggling to pay my mortgage or that my brother is suicidal?

'This bloke is the lone wolf. And what he really needs is a mate who says, "You don't look so good, you should go and see a doctor."

'Do you,' Mike asks the room, 'have someone who says, "Mate, those thought patterns of yours don't sound very healthy. You should get some help with that"? Do you have someone who says, "Hey, mate, she didn't think that was funny. Knock it off"?'

It's a true pin-drop moment.

'It's all about support, and it's about accountability, and sometimes we think those two things are different. Support without accountability is weak. And accountability without support is, frankly, just unhelpful. I think we need to hold men to account with kindness and compassion and empathy and, dare I say it, love.'

The only thing missing from this room filled with Water Corporation employees are some grey-haired blokes from management for whom it should probably matter most. The rest of this crew, young men and women, are lapping it up. Understanding it without discomfort. Listening closely. Generationally aware.

With a small, slightly self-conscious smile, Mike mentions that his dad didn't tell him he loved him 'until I was about eighteen'. He doesn't dwell on it or break into floods of tears or suggest we hold hands and sing 'Kumbaya' – he just sharpens his message even further.

'Lone Wolf Syndrome is a vicious cycle which prevents us from being part of the solution. Our job as men is to talk more openly, connect with other blokes and say, "Hey, what are we actually going to do about it?"

Why We Have to Work at Friendships

We need to check in more proactively with each other. Hold each other to account. Have their backs. Be a real mate.'

With that, the audience applauds, and Mike grins back at them. Thankful of the opportunity. He'll be back again in the new year to hold further workshops. I take my leave at this point.

It dawns on me later that I never found out how Mike broke his ribs. And I'm curious to know. So I send him a text.

He replies: 'It's a story of high adventure and bravery. I tripped over my own undies changing my pants in a campground car park. Fell onto a parking bollard and landed on the ground with my pants around my ankles. And with two broken ribs.'

Mike is clearly what he promises to help us become – a good bloke. Honest, accountable and unafraid to be vulnerable. A terrific mate.

Are you a good one? There's still time to get better at it.

Chapter 10

Talking Footy

My Australian boyhood was dominated by sport. It meant everything. On a Saturday morning, I'd listen to footy from Melbourne on our local ABC Radio station, 6WF, while kicking a Burley around the back lawn, selling the dummy to invisible defenders and snapping 'Don't tell me he's kicked it?' goals over my shoulder. Then it was inside for a cheese and tomato sandwich.

But it was cricket I loved best, and when Australia toured England, I had the tranny (that's 'transistor radio') under the pillow, listening through the foggy drift of night as commentators described the incredible unfolding drama at Lord's, where Bob Massie took sixteen wickets on debut. So began a lifelong love of both the wireless and faraway places, kindled by the soft burr of John Arlott painting word pictures about things beyond the game – the imminent arrival of trains and the inevitability of rain.

Then there was my equine hero, Gunsynd. The Goondiwindi Grey. One Saturday morning, celebrating another of his race wins, nine-year-old me ran down the hallway, which had now become the straight at Moonee

Valley, shouting 'Mum! Dad! He's won! He's won!' before clipping a skirting board, hitting the wall and splitting my head open. I still wear that massive dent with pride. It pulses like Gunsynd's magnificent heart when life excites me or I have too much to drink.

And as I understand life today, sport is still the preferred language and cultural pastime of Australian men. Safe territory. Easy conversation that requires little more of us than the willingness to express loud, heartfelt and often splendidly uninformed opinions.

We take sides and barrack hard. We rib those who aren't part of our tribe, and we taunt and isolate those who either know nothing or, worse, pretend they're experts. It can be cruel and unwelcoming to outsiders, but it also satisfies our never-actually-had-to-fight-in-a-war impulses. It's also great fun.

We sit in pubs staring up at big screens, or bet on which player will kick the first goal, or engage in furiously contested debates where we evaluate athletes and teams from different generations in ludicrous, unanswerable hypotheticals.

We love sport. And as I hinted in the previous chapter, I reckon sometimes we talk about it just to fill the gaps that might otherwise require us to publicly consider other things. Like what's really going on in our lives. And how we feel about stuff. And what our mental health is like. And what might be gnawing away at us.

And I can hear the response above the pub chatter: 'Fuck off, mate. If I need an analyst, I'll make an appointment.'

Eyes turn back to the big screen.

When I was a kid, footy was a game played on sodden, muddy grounds in winter by tough, uncompromising men. It was better then. Ask anyone of a certain age and they'll probably get all misty-eyed and start talking about suburban clubs, player loyalty and the simple beauty of mark, kick, goal and smack around the head. About Saturday afternoons, standing on beer cans in the outer, eating pies and shouting out whatever you damn well liked.

And there again lies that magnificent nostalgic grievance that entices us as we blokes get older and the world rushes past. Footy doesn't seem to be as good as it used to be. The game has changed. We hate that they – and 'they' is some dark, unaccountable bureaucracy – keep tinkering with the rules. We're told it's meant to make the game faster and more spectacular; instead, it's become confusing, technical and impossible to officiate. But we hate umpires even more.

And we always loved 'a bit of biffo', but that too has been removed because it now carries the medical consequence of traumatic brain injury or the legal consequence of common assault.

And if only players would 'Just bloody kick it' instead of weaving tactical threads backwards and across the ground before looking for space in the corridor.

And all the while, swarms of desperate, kill-their-mothers-to-get-a-story journos fight each other for gossip and rumour and exclusive pics of some cocky kid appearing to snort cocaine off a toilet seat.

Those players used to have jobs. And work in banks or as plumbers.

What was once pretty simple, is now very complicated. Ruined. Sport as a microcosm of life.

~

And if you agree that any part of this is true, do you ever wonder what life is like for the newer version of you, of us, who play the game? What is footy to them in this era where a poor personal performance might be accompanied not just by your disappointment as a fan, but also by a death threat on their Instagram page when they get home?

These boys are our sons and grandsons. And the next time we furiously demand they 'Just bloody kick it' or declare 'That useless prick is hopeless', might it be worth wondering what it's like to be a young bloke trying his guts out under our furious critical gaze?

Well, I'm about to ask Fremantle Dockers captain Alex Pearce. He's agreed to meet me at Percy Flint's, a local watering hole in the People's Republic of South Fremantle, where we both live.

Originally from Tasmania, Alex came to Fremantle when he was still a teenager. Now, at twenty-nine, having battled serious leg injuries for years and had long periods out of the game feeling pretty depressed about it all, he's a brilliant and courageous defender and an outstanding leader on and off the field. He is also very tall and hairy and today arrives with a curly mane stuffed under a beanie.

I am grateful and surprised Alex has agreed to yet another media request, but he seems to like the premise of the book. He's a thinker, this man, maybe even an overthinker. When he's not trying to nullify a key forward each week, he's working to complete a degree in psychology and politics.

I buy him a non-alcoholic beer and ask him about the game he plays and what the environment around it looks like today, compared to his arrival in 2013.

He takes off his beanie. Honestly, his hair cascades like a theatre curtain enveloping a stage.

'Back then, you probably had to conform more to what the status quo was. At one stage, guys were getting told to shave their beards. And tattoos were sort of frowned upon. And piercings were frowned upon. Whereas now, I'm the captain and I've got my nose pierced, I've got my nipple pierced. I've got my long hair. And we've got guys who have cornrows in and they change their hairstyles every week. The group is a lot more multicultural now than when I first came in. And I do think it's important that everyone's allowed to express themselves and be who they are.'

Alex's story is deeply textured and he's still working through it.

'I'm still a pretty self-conscious guy. And I get social anxiety when I come into places and I see people looking at me.'

I ask him why.

'I used to be really uncomfortable about my Aboriginality, my ancestry, because I'm a white guy who has Indigenous roots in Tasmania. And I didn't know a lot about it, but always knew this was my history and heritage. It comes through my paternal grandmother and can be traced back to the Aboriginal warrior Mannalargenna and Dolly Dalrymple, who were both prominent figures in early colonial Tasmanian Indigenous history.

'And then when I came here, I saw a very strong Indigenous culture and people are very connected to their culture and their families, and I wasn't. And you cop a little bit of shit for being the white dude who's a part of that group. And I really, really struggled. It would keep me up at night because I knew what some of the comments would be. "Wow. Look at this boy trying to get attention," or "What's he trying to get out of it?" And I had to grapple with it, and it took me a while. And now I'm still not a hundred per cent comfortable.'

It's not surprising. Alex is exploring his identity in an Australia where too many people carry this miserable invalidating suspicion, unable or unwilling to cede anything to First Nations people. As my friend the acclaimed Indigenous psychologist Dr Tracy Westerman pointed out to me recently, 'Our authenticity is always being challenged. No one ever asks how Chinese or Greek you are.'

Add that complication to the fact that professional athletes like Alex do much of their growing up in public. When your privacy is not your own, the search for an authentic self can be challenging, particularly when a stranger feels entitled to snap your image and put it on TikTok without your permission. Every decision you make, every representation of self that becomes public, really matters.

Sometimes the motivation of others is pure fandom; sometimes it is more vindictive. Alex and the other young men we cheer and jeer at have to live with both our adoration and scorn.

'A hundred per cent, even when you brought this beer over, I was like, "Oh, jeez. I wish you brought this in a can, so that everyone could see it was not alcoholic."'

'Really?' I ask.

'Yeah, I am guarded about what people think, because lots of them do have opinions on what I should do, and how I should play or how I should act.

'I do feel really privileged as well. And I guess I grapple with working through these things, whilst also not complaining too much about the situation and the cards that I've been dealt, because I'm very aware that I've been dealt an amazing hand in life.'

At this point, I show Alex a newly published picture of three Freo players – Brandon Walker, Josh Draper and Michael Frederick – in the rooms after the game. Walker was born in Ghana, Draper's mother was a refugee from Ethiopia and Frederick's parents are from South Sudan. They have taken off their jumpers and are sitting with big smiles, their hands on each other's knees. They ripple and glisten and shine.

Alex laughs at the photo. I then read one of the comments that accompanied it on social media. It comes from a bloke named Ian, who is clearly a barrel of laughs.

'Maybe I'm showing my age, but back when I played footy, we would get the shit kicked out of us for posing like that. Anyway, just as long as they keep playing well, I guess.'

I ask Alex how he hears Ian's words.

'It's not a representation or a reflection of the photo. It's a reflection of the person who's making that comment. It's probably a little …'

'Homoerotic for Ian?' I offer.

'Yeah.'

~

I've tried to understand Ian's comment, just like Old Coot's, and it still puzzles me. Why did he even bother to add his miserable opinion to a post that was filled with good humour and kind support for these players?

To be provocative? Nice one, Ian. It worked. I think you're a cynical, mean-spirited dickhead. But that's just me.

The only real conclusion I can draw is that he only respects these young men when they are winning. His contempt is one fumble or miskick away. And I don't say that lightly.

Many of you will remember back in 1993 when St Kilda great Nicky Winmar lifted his jumper and pointed to his skin, declaring 'I'm proud to be black' in an act of defiance against Collingwood fans who had racially abused him and teammate Gilbert McAdam. I was working for the Nine Network's *Wide World of Sports* at the time, and a couple of days later managed to get the only interview with Collingwood president Allan McAlister, which would air on our flagship program, *Sports Sunday*.

When I asked him what he thought of the behaviour of Collingwood fans and whether he realised how offensive the remarks were to Winmar, he declared he had no issue with Indigenous footballers. 'As long as they conduct themselves like white people, well, off the field, everyone will admire and respect ... as long as they conduct themselves like human beings, they will be alright.' Thirty years later the club finally apologised to Nicky Winmar for the hurt caused.

Ian just sounds a bit like Allan McAlister to me.

I wonder what he'd think of Alex's nipple piercing. Or the fact Freo's captain attended Pride Day earlier in the year.

'Yeah, I posted a photo, and had some rainbow paint on my face, and we had the rainbow flag. And it was an interesting experience. I felt a little bit uncomfortable being there as a straight man, but I was proud in a way to help represent the community of Freo supporters, and our women's players who were part of that queer community. But yeah, I had some comments on there from people, just like, I don't know ...'

His voice trails away.

~

Alex recently lost one of his best friends to suicide. And private grief was to be played out in the most public setting.

Cam McCarthy was a superbly gifted footballer and an ebullient personality who first went to the Greater Western Sydney Giants before coming home to Fremantle. He enjoyed some success, but in 2020, after forty-nine games, Fremantle announced that his contract would not be renewed. He drifted a little in the years that followed – whatever that observation really means – and in May 2024, hours before Fremantle was due to play Sydney in front of a big Friday-night television audience, the news emerged that McCarthy had been found unresponsive at his home.

That night, while we in the stadium looked on, Alex Pearce stood with his arm around champion teammate Nat Fyfe and stared up at the big screen paying tribute to their friend. The pair wept.

It was so raw. And so heartbreakingly sad. And today I ask if he despaired of that moment and the responsibility it demanded.

'No. Not at all. For a while during that day, I didn't think it would be possible to play. But once the visceral outpouring of emotion had calmed, I began to think, "What would Cam want me to do?" I asked myself, "What is my bond with him?" And it was forged a lot through football. And even recently, when he wasn't playing, he would speak to me a lot, just fill me with praise, "You're doing this," and "You're so good," and "You're going to be All Australian this year. I love you so much." And it was like, well, I have to play, because he would want me to play.'

Alex explains, a little red-eyed now, of the importance of honouring his friend. Which he did again, just a fortnight later, at a crucial moment against Collingwood in a game where Fremantle stormed home to secure a last-minute draw.

'That day, I was able to take a mark and kick a goal to bring us back into it, and have this moment [where he thrust his right arm skyward] and then speak about it in front of a national audience and cry and show some vulnerability. And it's like, it was just aligned perfectly.'

Here in front of me is a bloke, notionally a younger Millennial, who can find words, trust his heart and not fear the vulnerability of speaking a personal truth. And again I feel privileged. I see a more evolved Aussie bloke than I was at that age. Perhaps you too.

It makes me feel hopeful for our sons and grandsons. Or the young man who your granddaughter or grandson nervously introduces you to ahead of a school ball. If we can free them up a little to explore who they are – and yes, I love the phrase 'authentic self' – and we don't assume too much about the person they should be or the roles they should play, if we can resist that willingness to project our prejudices and insecurities onto them, then I'm convinced we will get to be part of something important and good. The evolution of ever more interesting and generous and kind versions of us.

Does that make sense to you?

I don't say this aloud to Alex. I think he instinctively knows it.

What about his dad?

'He's a pretty stereotypical dad. Enjoys sport, drinking beer, loves his family. Probably doesn't show it in the best ways at times, but in certain crises, or when you need him, he would be there, for sure. We definitely have similarities around our love of sport. And that has always bonded us and kept us close. When we chat on the phone, which isn't as often as it should be, it's mainly around sport. And that's our language to communicate.'

Alex pauses.

'And I do worry about him as well. And over these next two weeks, I actually want to have a really deep chat with him around all this.

'Is he happy? I think a lot about my own happiness, and understanding it, and knowing what I need to be happy. Whereas, I do wonder about the older generation, how much they think about, "Am I happy?"'

I tell Alex that this is the very question I asked my dad nearly half a century ago.

As we finish up, I ask him what he thinks blokes like me and his dad might learn from their sons and grandsons. What, indeed, might make us less prone to being grumpy?

'To me, I just think they need to be curious and be open to difference. Difference is fine. Difference is great. And you should be open to learn about difference, and why people think the way they do, and why they act like they act.

'So, for instance, when they see or hear about trans issues and go, "Oh, it's fucking ridiculous. Fucking stupid. Back in my day ..." – all that does is ensure that you are going to be angry whenever the issue comes up. Why not be educated and empathetic? Because everyone's happier when they're more empathetic.

'We are all humans. And that community isn't trying to hurt anyone else and take things away from anyone else. They're trying to be happy, and feel safe, and feel valued. And that's what we're all trying to do, just like the old guy sitting on his couch wants to feel safe, wants to feel valued as well.'

Safe and valued. Curious and open to difference.

I think I'm going to get my nipple pierced.

Chapter 11

Secret Sorrows

Do you remember your wedding day?

We got married at the Melbourne Zoo, and it says something not entirely flattering about me that my overwhelming memory of the time as Phillipa and I posed for photographs is being serenaded by whooping orangutans while they masturbated in the tree canopy high above our heads. I thought they were cheering.

We have since accumulated thirty-two years together and a couple of kids and have lived in lots of different places. And I am grateful for everything.

I am also aware that, should the contract be broken – and yes, all our friends would be shocked – they'd also immediately side with Phillipa and abandon me, even if it was she who committed the heinous marriage-ending crime. Why? Because everyone I know likes my wife more than me. And they, including the kids, would assume that whatever caused her to go mad with an axe was probably my fault.

So keep that in mind if you are being really grumpy and your behaviour is having an impact on your relationship. Should it come down to taking sides, no one will choose to be on yours. That's just how it is.

Because our partners are usually much nicer than we are. And more generous. And more sensitive to the needs of others.

Is that an air-raid siren going off in the background?

~

As mentioned in Chapter 3, grey divorce is on the rise. Almost a third of all divorces are now taking place among the over-fifties.

Further to that, consumer research group CoreData, on behalf of Australian Seniors insurance, recently asked more than 1200 Australians over the age of fifty how they're dealing with the aftermath of divorce, and it seems 57 per cent are content to be on their own. They ended the relationship for a multitude of reasons, but did so because most of them want to put their personal happiness first.

That tells us something about the changing societal attitudes to divorce. It's less a terrible stigma, more the opportunity to have a new life. If you no longer feel safe or happy in your marriage, Australian society no longer dictates you have to stay.

So how's it working out for those who choose to leave? Apparently, 73 per cent are enjoying additional personal space, 72 per cent are enjoying greater independence and 63 per cent are positively delighting in the peace and quiet. For the women, perhaps that's the peace and quiet of not listening to us? For all those who are now newly single, women are much more comfortable about staying that way than men are. They don't need or want to be attached anymore.

That's something Mum noticed when she went to live in a retirement village. The women were often relieved to be by themselves. The blokes?

Fellas like Handsy Harry and Smooth-Talking Sam, now closer to eighty than not, were still on the lookout for a new partner to make a nice light supper and wash their undies. The ladies, generally, recoiled.

No surprise then that when the figures came out, *The Sydney Morning Herald* was very clear in its headline: 'All the single ladies: Why more women over 50 are going solo and loving it!'

Now, of course, there are many men instigating grey divorce too and seeking the same benefits: the chance of a new beginning, unencumbered by the burden of the past, and perhaps some peace and quiet. But we should make no mistake. Unless we work on this relationship, or are prepared to adjust our behaviour at times, it won't survive in a meaningful way.

We'd do well to understand that, today, our partners have options. And increasingly they take the option to leave.

CoreData's research also tells us the average Australian couple over fifty has been together for thirty-four years, and three in four of those interviewed said they're facing challenges in that relationship. Nearly four in ten have doubts about it continuing. There's lots at stake.

But we're in this together, right? We're sweet, aren't we?

Why is she looking at me like that?

So here's just one question to consider, albeit loaded with other questions. Are there things you carry with you that are hurting and eroding your most intimate relationships? A secret or a sadness that might explain why you have developed such a jaundiced and suspicious view of the world?

And if you don't know what I'm getting at, or are just pretending not to … consider these words from the nineteenth-century American poet

Henry Wadsworth Longfellow, who despite his silly middle name was clearly a sensitive new-age guy: 'Believe me, every heart has its secret sorrows which the world knows not, and oftentimes we call a man cold, when he is only sad.'

Henry nailed the problem that has been making men sad forever. The inability to share.

So, back to that uncomfortable question. Do you carry such secrets? And could you, would you, be prepared to talk to your partner about it? Rather than continue to conceal the source of this unhappiness, might you try to find the words to describe what brought you to this irritated, ill-tempered and sad place? Of underlying trauma. Or deep anxiety.

Spoken. Out loud. And perhaps for the first time.

It's a bit frightening to consider, isn't it? To open yourself up.

And I bet some of you are thinking, "What if I reveal too much? What if she … What if she laughs at me? What if she discovers who I really am? And what if she doesn't like me anymore?"

~

I think my dad had lots of secrets and regrets, about which we will speak later.

There are reasons why we bury the unhappy parts of ourselves; that way, they can't escape to hurt us. They can't be discovered, to embarrass us and cause us shame. But clamping down the lid and nailing it shut doesn't stop them churning away in our head, heart and guts, corroding our ability to laugh and love and be at ease.

And even as I write these lines, they feel a bit close to the bone, because I think this unspoken inner turmoil and profound sorrow lay deep within Dad. And he never shared it. So we could never really know him. Or be of help.

I don't want to lock myself up like that. I don't want to have so little faith in the world and the people around me that I can't talk to them or ask for some help. And I don't want you to be that lone wolf either.

So what would happen if you, me and us sat down in front of our partners and tried to tell a deeply personal truth? What do you think would happen?

~

Maggie Dent, commonly known as the 'Queen of Common Sense', is a bestselling parenting author, a men's counsellor, a wife and the proud mother of four sons. She knows and understands blokes well and works hard to help us live better lives. She's quite the fan.

So, over coffee and a slightly stale cheese and chive muffin, I go looking for her insights. I'm not even sure how to phrase my question in anything but a convoluted way.

'Maggie, if a bloke summons the courage to speak up about his unhappiness or the secrets he might have kept for years, what kind of a response might he get?' I don't give her a chance to answer. I want to qualify it further. 'We know he fears ridicule and has been told for most of his life that any such revelation is weakness. What can he expect a partner to say?'

She looks at me from behind her black-rimmed glasses and lays out some ground rules.

'Geoff, presuming this is a safe, respectful relationship and assuming he's going to reveal that he's been finding life hard lately, or his moods are getting dark, or his anger is worrying him, or he's worried the black dog of depression won't leave him alone – assuming that is the essence of this conversation, then overwhelmingly the woman he loves will step forward. She will not step back.'

I almost gasp when I hear this. Perhaps out of relief. Maggie doesn't mess around with this stuff. She believes it. Profoundly.

I ask, 'How can you be so sure?'

She explains, 'The fact is, the expression of emotional honesty in our intimate relationships opens the heart. Simple as that. Not only will his partner want to help him, I have seen so many women become like a lioness. They will step forward and cover their man's back and collaborate and work with their man to ensure he gets the help he needs. Because there is so much at stake and the need is enormous.'

Maggie has something of the lioness about her too. She is speaking from long experience.

'I have worked with men who have lived with trauma,' she says. 'It might be deep grief following the childhood death of a parent or it might be an experience of sexual violence or molestation. Those men have been silent for more than thirty to forty years because they feel such profound shame. Some of them have endured incredibly painful experiences from their boyhood. They were often belted or punished severely, and to this day may still not know what they did wrong, what was supposedly so bad. And they've kept it all a secret. Out of fear the woman they love will no longer be able to love and respect them.

'Think about it, Geoff. Is it any wonder that when you have something big and terrible in your past, you're going to be a grumpy man? Is it any wonder that you might drink and fight and have difficulty controlling your anger? You have a wound. And, Geoff, I can tell you, it is a wound that needs light.'

I pick at what's left of my muffin. Maggie makes it sound simple and provable, like a mathematic formula. Expression of emotional honesty = an open heart and a happy resolution. She believes we just have to give ourselves permission to search for and find and then speak those words of emotional honesty. Out loud. To someone else.

And I wonder: hearing this, do you believe this could be true for you? And if so, is there someone in your life who would listen and understand and act on your behalf? And would you allow them to see inside your heart? And be that lioness?

I'll let that sit.

There are times in our lives we need help. There are times we may well be too scared or too bloody stubborn to ask for it. But there is a sensitivity and fragility in us that needs to be recognised.

Right now, I know of a handful of blokes, good friends of mine, who as they get closer to sixty seem to be stumbling towards a cliff. Losing balance and perspective. It might be alcoholism, financial despair or that very real sense that after all this time, life is only going to get harder for them. And the world seems a more unsympathetic place now.

Some of them will veer away from the edge. Some will be able to cope. To reset and go again. But others may seem increasingly unable to find the resolve they need or the instincts they formerly relied upon. And they may yet risk losing their homes and families.

What happens then? Is there someone we can talk to? Reveal ourselves to?

If the answer is yes and if we can do so, without the self-sabotage of thinking that it represents weakness or failure or shame, then surely we stand a pretty good chance of getting through the hardest bits.

And the payoff?

Imagine it. The worst of that burden of regret and sorrow might be lifted from our shoulders. And suddenly there would be room for better. Maggie calls it 'rediscovering our capacity for joy'.

Anyway. You've read this far. Like everything else in this handbook, the ideas are just here for your consideration.

You may still ponder, 'Why is she looking at me like that?'

The answer, I think, is that she loves you. And she wants life to be easier. For you.

And for her. And the kids.

So do the orangutans. Look at them up in the trees … they're cheering you on.

Chapter 12

Your Sexual Health

From the moment we boys arrive kicking and screaming into this world, it seems we want to conquer it. And the weapon we like to latch onto and wave about until someone tells us to 'Stop that right now!' is perched between our ham and eggs and just above the Jatz crackers.

It can lie there dormant and slug-like or it can fill with bloody stupid notions of world domination.

But our penises are fascinating things, aren't they?

I hope you don't mind, but the use of euphemism of the male sex organ has, to my mind, served us no benefit apart from sparing people a few blushes and infantilising any attempt to talk seriously about our relationship with it. How are we equipped to take a lifetime of responsibility for our penis if we can't even call it by its real name?

So, no references to pee-pees here or Barry McKenzie pointing Percy at the porcelain or any waving about of a one-eyed trouser snake. Okay?

Definitely no pork swords.

That's the problem, you see. Blokes generally don't like talking about sexual health unless it is to lie about our prowess or make space-filling jokes to hide our deep embarrassment.

Not all of us are embarrassed, of course. I well remember a blistering summer day in suburban Melbourne when I, a newly married man, did what newly married men do ...

No, not that.

I had the old Victa roaring out on the verge, ricocheting gravel around patchy scraps of couch grass. Living the dream, I was. Apropos of nothing, our friendly-to-the-point-of-being-overfamiliar neighbour Jim waddled by for a yarn and to say helpful things like, 'I love watching people work. I could stay here and do it for hours.'

Jim was an unmarried former merchant seaman, and on this day the crusty seventy-four-year-old suddenly became the teenage sailor he once was as he navigated the Strait of Malacca or wherever he set his sail and for some reason made mention of the enormous erections he was able to pluck from seemingly nowhere while out at sea. I have forgotten nearly everything Jim ever told me, but I have never forgotten this.

'You coulda hung a wet towel off it,' he said dreamily. 'A wet towel!' Before picking a couple of lemons and heading home over the road to his sister Mary.

Thanks for that, Jim. A reminder, perhaps, that there is a big difference between the effortless flag-raising virility of your teenage years and the decades that follow.

The fact is, this life makes us warriors wilt. And it is testosterone or a lack of it that lies at the core of those challenges most of us would prefer not to talk about. So with that in mind ...

Just as we have discussed so many things that seem to go wrong with our bodies as we get older and what we can do about them or choose not to do about them, I think we should spend a few moments talking about how we deal with a decline in our libido and our sense of manhood.

Let's meet one of Australia's foremost men's sexual health experts, Dr Michael.

Do we have to?

Yes. I have much to ask him on your behalf.

Dr Michael seems a lovely man. He's seventy-three years old, has no intention of retiring any time soon and from our Zoom chat I can tell he has a gentle bedside manner. He also appears to have very soft hands. I don't know why I've told you this, but I imagine soft hands are a requirement for his job.

~

Dr Michael, thank you for taking the time to talk to me. I wonder if we can begin by establishing, right from the start, just how many readers of this book may be experiencing some form of sexual dysfunction?

'Plenty of them, Geoff. At fifty years of age, we know that 50 per cent of men will have a sexual problem – not total lack of erection, but a problem. At sixty, it will be 60 per cent. At seventy, it will be 70 per cent ... As you age, your testosterone drops, and you are not as horny as you were when you were younger and you will struggle to get and hold an erection. This is a really natural part of ageing in men.'

Okay, so declining testosterone may be a natural part of the ageing process, but I have to ask what's actually happening ... down there?

At this point, I feel the need to nod towards my lap. Just in case he doesn't understand.

He smiles patiently.

'The ability to reach a climax becomes more difficult because the dorsal nerve of the penis, the one that supplies sensation to the end of the penis, becomes a little less sensitive with age, and it's not uncommon for older men to say they really struggle to climax. And while they struggle to climax, they get anxious and lose their erection, leading to all sorts of problems.'

I assure him I'm not asking for the names of celebrities or former prime ministers, but I do want to know who comes to see Dr Michael. He begins to tick off the category of clients.

'We have the older guy who partners with a much younger person and he wants to behave like he did thirty years ago, particularly because he is worried that his partner won't be satisfied. I also see young men in their twenties who have terrible performance anxiety, because of pressure from their peers, or a partner who might make a negative comment and that really fucks them up.

'On top of it all, I've seen a lot of men who have either benign prostate disease that impacts on bladder function, or prostate cancer. We know BPH – benign prostatic hyperplasia – and erectile dysfunction just go hand in hand. Whenever I see a man with prostate symptoms, it's inevitable he's got an erection problem.

'That's the stuff I deal with.'

I have lots of questions. I can't stop asking these questions.

What form does an examination take? Do you invite the patient to talk about his sexual history or do you know much of that in advance? How do you frame delicate conversations? Do you spare his blushes or speak frankly? Will you ask him about his relationship with his mother? Do some patients come in with their mothers?

Dr Michael must have dealt with some idiots down the years. He knows one when he sees one. He sighs.

'Geoff, I have no prior knowledge of their sexual history, so I follow my standard routine and get straight to the point. I do take a full social history. I never blush. When these guys come to see me, it is pretty much understood about the depth of the visit.'

I don't want Dr Michael to think I'm an idiot. But ...

Is there a physical examination? Do you put on rubber gloves, warm up your hands and then ask the patient to drop his trousers?

'Physical examination may or may not occur. Depends on a number of factors. I am interested in weight, blood pressure, waist circumference, size of testes and penile scarring or foreskin issues. If appropriate, I check the prostate.'

You say you treat, not cure. Can you explain what we need to be realistic about?

'I aim for a "good enough" erection, not a perfect one nor necessarily a cure. I follow very much a treating medical model. If the guy is unlucky enough to have prostate cancer – and the surgery is very good these days – it's inevitable that he will have either permanent or temporary erectile dysfunction after the surgery. I treat these guys; I do their sexual rehabilitation.'

~

I know this all sounds a bit serious, but Dr Michael hastens to add that, for us blokes, our testosterone levels fall very slowly from the age of about thirty, but this decline occurs so slowly we barely recognise it and we are able to adjust accordingly. Not so with women and menopause, a much more dramatic event, where hormones drop suddenly.

But if we are overweight, if we have a poor diet and high cholesterol and if we have sleep apnoea or diabetes or coronary artery disease or combinations of all or some, we are particularly vulnerable.

Does that sound like you? Me neither.

Pauses.

Walks down hall of mirrors. Has a good look.

Dr Michael then mentions what this kind of sexual dysfunction is called. It's a strength-sapping, blood-draining, life-softening term – hypogonadism.

I wander off later for a second opinion, and the boffins at the Mayo Clinic, one of the world's leading medical research facilities, sum it up succinctly. But not nicely.

Decreased sex drive. Decreased energy. Depression.

And over time, men with hypogonadism can develop …

Erectile dysfunction. Infertility. A decrease in hair growth on the face and body. Decrease in muscle mass. Development of breast tissue. Loss of bone mass.

And on it goes.

So it is no surprise that we men start to feel less secure about who we are and what we are capable of, sexually – because we risk going bald, developing man boobs and feeling like a weakling. We are becoming everything we have been programmed not to become.

And our very sense of self sags.

In case you're curious.

For men with prostate-related issues, sexual rehabilitation may involve oral medications, penile injections, a vacuum erection device and a pump discreetly hidden inside your Jatz crackers.

I will not speak in any more detail here of those matters.

As for the rest of us? Well, you can't say we haven't been told all this before.

So, Dr Michael, what can we do about it? Or at least mitigate the impact of it?

'Losing weight and exercising and eating better will not only help your lifestyle, it may improve your sexual function. It might mean Viagra will work better, if you are fitter. As I tell my patients, I can't cure you, but I can treat you.'

And just on that, Dr Michael. What if I don't want to do any of these things? What if I think you mainstream medicine practitioners are of course all stooges of Big Pharma and merely doing the bidding of our Lizard Overlords, who wish to stupefy us into sheeple-like submission?

I don't actually ask Dr Michael this.

Though I do ask him ...

Can't I just take a pill? Or click a piece of email spam that promises (I start reading) that I too will be able to increase my 'penis length and girth for longer erections while improving the sensitivity of orgasm for better sex!' What's more, it says, categorically, 'I can be cured of my sexual difficulties and regain my sexual power in four seconds! Not three or five, but four.'

I'm beginning to shout. I'm having a lovely time.

Dr Michael isn't laughing.

'That advertisement, Geoff, is typical of all the rubbish claims for sexual enhancement. The problem is it draws vulnerable men. It may well be sildenafil in disguise, like Kamagra.'

I nod, but don't really understand.

After, I do a little research. There's a reason for his disdain. In 2021, Australia's Therapeutic Goods Administration issued a formal warning about the use of illegal erectile-dysfunction pills. And while we might be tempted to try products with super sexy names like Panther Power Platinum 11000 or One Night Love, the TGA declared that they are a 'serious risk' to health and should not be taken.

Why? It is unknown what they actually contain, but they may have, as Dr Michael observed, sildenafil, which, yes, is used to treat erectile dysfunction, but can, according to the TGA, interact with nitrogen compounds found in some drugs and lower blood pressure to dangerous levels. Nitrates are often prescribed to people with coronary artery disease, while amyl nitrite is taken as a recreational drug. So don't go there, kids, even if they promise you'll go off like a bottle of French fizz.

~

I hope this hasn't terrified you. I hope you were able to read beyond phrases like 'penile injections'.

But Dr Michael also has an interesting observation about what we can do right now – to perhaps help mitigate some of these problems as we age.

'I work with a cardiologist, and I don't think we are aggressive enough with heart disease. He reckons every man at fifty should have a calcium score of the state of his heart. Because it gives you a very good prediction of the risk. I think it's really important that we maximise our cardiovascular health.'

And that was a fascinating coincidence. Just days after our interview, I was booked in to have that very procedure. A CT scan that will tell me how much calcified plaque there is in my arteries. A simple risk assessment for coronary artery disease. I'll detail my experience in a moment.

My last question to Dr Michael is a personal one.

What makes you grumpy?

'When I don't get my way, I can get grumpy. I like things to be just right and perfect, and I get grumpy if things don't go my way. I just need everything to be ordered, in a very Germanic sort of way.'

Chapter 12 and a Bit

Keeping the Calcium Score

The radiological clinic waiting room is packed, filled with amiable older folk who are used to sitting in these places and a young woman who clearly is not – apologising profusely to the receptionist on the other side of the glass for having left her documentation at home. I sit in a tiny booth. There is a hum of high-tech medical examination all around me and the gentle slap of sandal on vinyl as staff hurry back and forth.

I can hear the conversations clearly through thin walls.

'Have you had a back injury recently?'

'And no caffeine or exercise in the last four hours?'

'Someone will come for you shortly.'

I am invited into a room for a CT scan.

I lie on my back in my undies, with my arms tucked behind my head. There are five adhesive strips on my chest, attached to wires that trail beyond my view. The mechanism moves me feet first into the mouth of the machine. A disembodied voice from a bad 1950s sci-fi movie tells me, 'Breathe in and hold.'

Everything but me starts to spin. I am an unmoving figure within a chaotic, bucking clothes dryer.

I am moved out of the machine. And then moved in again. 'Breathe in and hold.'

And then I am released. It has taken no more than five minutes, and this simple procedure may tell my doctor what my medical future looks like. What Dr Michael calls the state of my heart.

When the results are in, I go and see my GP.

I won't lie to you; I get nervous waiting for numbers to be read out.

First up, he explains what's behind them.

'Geoff, your coronary artery calcium score gives us an idea of the blockage burden of the arteries supplying oxygen to the heart muscle. It helps to stratify your risk of heart disease and determine how aggressive we need to be with your treatments.'

So what were the results?

'Your score of sixty-five puts you right at the average for men your age. It shows early signs of blockage, but they're not likely to be related to significant issues with blood flow. What we'll do is increase your cholesterol medications, to aim for tighter control, which can stop any further blockage over time.'

Effectively, my statin dose is to rise from twenty milligrams to forty milligrams. That's it.

If I continue to eat well, don't drink too much and get good exercise, I should be in pretty decent shape.

It didn't hurt, it wasn't scary and I'm booked in for next year.

Chapter 13

No Excuse for Violence

'If you're yelling at your wife and she's not yelling back – is that an argument? No, that's just you being a dickhead.'

Rob Andrew, family-violence counsellor

Last Friday night, my wife and I went to pick up a pizza. I drive; she collects. The operation requires almost-military precision to ensure we take delivery of the diavola just moments after it's shovelled from the oven. The crust needs to be crisp; the salami needs to be bubbling. But the plan only works if we are lucky enough to pinch a parking spot. Hard to do in a crowded street.

I thought I'd found one, before realising it was only designated for motorcycles. After taking a moment or two to reset, and with surely no more than five seconds of peering uncertainty, I was suddenly stunned by an explosion of invective.

'Make up your fucking mind, you fucking stupid c%#t!'

It was a ferocious verbal slap. I turned my head to see where it came from, expecting some hi-vis tradie in a huge ute. But no ...

It was a cyclist. An old bloke. Older than me.

Sorry about the assumption. They're convenient, but dangerous and often wrong. And we use them all the time.

He reared away at speed, shaking his fist.

I was taken aback. I tried to imagine how I'd inconvenienced him or placed him at any risk, given traffic had slowed to a crawl and there were cautious pedestrians everywhere. Maybe he was just in a hurry to get home. To berate his partner. Or kick the dog.

We drove home with our pizza.

~

I seem to be thinking about this bloke a lot. Let's call him Lycra Larry.

He was hidden under a helmet, so I will probably never recognise him in the street or share another moment with him. But I have found it hard to understand why he was so angry and why he appeared to have so little control over that anger. And how, for a few moments, his anger shook me up.

I wonder who was waiting for him at home that night. And whether he'd cooled off and parked his outrage with his bike. I hope so.

Was Larry just having a bad day? Was my indecision just another sign of the idiocy that had marked his Friday? Was it a cyclist v. motorist thing? A road-rage reflex of fuck you?

And then I begin to ponder: what would he be like if he got really angry? And what would prompt it? A sideways look in a pub? A remark he disagreed with?

I really don't know anything about Lycra Larry, beyond the fact I made him grumpy. And he clearly accelerated past mild annoyance and barely contained frustration to absolute fury in the time it took me to say, 'A parking spot! Aah, it's only for motorbikes. Bugger.'

So here's the thing. If Lycra Larry went home and chose to go to the bathroom and do that look-in-the-mirror thing I suggested a few chapters ago, might he reflect not just on me, the idiot driver, but on the reason why he became so angry so quickly? Would he recognise his mood swings of late? How they seem to come from nowhere, grab him and then overwhelm him? Is he aware just how often he's been flying off the handle? And does he see how worried his partner is when he raises his voice? Or does he rationalise his outbursts by saying everything would be alright if people stopped giving him the absolute shits?

Maybe he stews on it. Or maybe he doesn't.

Maybe he just says, 'Ah well, it's all fucked anyway.' And switches off the light.

I'm guessing. I don't know him, and I don't understand anger very well. I have been shielded from it and largely safe from it and I don't like to express it, because I don't know where it will take me.

I recognise its validity. I understand it is a legitimate emotional expression of self. But should that red mist descend, I fear that loss of control.

And importantly, could I ever wrest back the consequences of my physicality or my words?

How about you?

~

I've just paraphrased all this in a conversation with my wife. She broadly agrees with my assessment but doesn't quite accept my selective memory.

'What about footy umpires? I've seen you very angry with them.'

Well, yes, but ...

But however conveniently I ignore it or downplay it or suggest 'that hardly counts', I know it's true. Because I think I know the particular moment to which she refers.

Fremantle v. Carlton, Round 12 in August 2021. With less than one minute to play, the Dockers had a two-point lead and were doggedly hanging on. And in those last seconds, three umpiring decisions would conspire to provide Carlton with a ludicrous, after-the-siren, shot-on-goal opportunity. The game was being stolen. And inexplicably, the final kick wouldn't even be taken by the player closest to the ball. A better player demanded and was given it.

I remember the red curtain descending and my brain on the verge of exploding. The miraculous goal was kicked. The humiliation complete. And I roared and booed and looked completely unhinged. And I walked back to the car alone. No one wanted to be with me.

And yet, as I picture those moments now, I'm reminded that there was something irresistible about those explosive seconds of outrage. I call it outrage because that implies some justification tied to it, yet I know there was none.

I'm trying to understand this.

I guess my reasoning in that moment – it is not reason, but let's go on – was that a great injustice was being inflicted on my team and by logical extension – it is not a logical extension – on all the good people of the Earth. I am entitled to protest on behalf of all those who have ever been wronged. Indeed, I must. Because life is so unfair.

~

Or I could just shut up. Accept the swings and roundabouts of footy and life and get it through my thick head that I'm not entitled to have everything go my way all the time.

Are you listening, fellow Boomers?

The truth is, it wasn't a poor umpiring decision that drove me to that sudden silly eruption. I chose not to be accountable for my behaviour. I chose to behave that way.

Just as Lycra Larry chose.

And the self-centred, red-faced ridiculousness of it all only became clear to me when my adult daughter poked me in the ribs and I felt her disappointment in me. And her awareness of my self-justifying privilege.

Male anger and violence have consequences far beyond aggressive language aimed at dopey drivers or football umpires. The statistics don't lie.

According to research group Counting Dead Women Australia, sixty-four women were killed in incidents of male violence in 2023. It should send a chill through us all that an organisation with that name even exists. The group keeps a daily total. Today, 25 September 2024, it reports that another forty-nine women have been killed this year.

And the Australian Institute of Health and Welfare confirms, 'While every experience of family, domestic or sexual violence is very personal and different, it is most common for this type of violence to be perpetrated against women, by men.'

Physical violence, sexual violence, emotional violence and coercive control. There are many behaviours and methods we men use to get what we want.

And it may not sound like you or me, but it is the story of us.

And Australia has a crisis on its hands.

We men are often told we are wired differently to women. That we have an inability to process our behaviour and our emotions or to find the words we need to express and understand them. That we lack impulse control – we're quick with our fists when we can't make sense of a world that does not bend to our will.

I don't think that's a description of me or my son. It wasn't true of my dad, and it's not of my brother or his son either. And I don't want good men to be damned by the behaviours of other men.

But such is the breadth and terrible consequence of male violence in Australia that it is surely on us to be in no doubt about the impact on partners and families and our broader community. On women and girls everywhere.

~

Today I read about a twenty-two-year-old woman who was killed in a Perth suburb, stabbed by a stranger in what police say was an unprovoked attack. A man, aged thirty, has been charged with murder.

When we hear such stories, our instinct is to feel sorrow, but then to turn away. It is all so unthinkably awful. And the news is so relentless and depressing. But right now, I don't want to turn away. I need to understand this is real. It's not a story. And if I have a regret about a career in journalism and broadcasting, it is the lens that reduces human experience to 'the story'.

And so, I've spent the last couple of hours thinking about this young woman and imagining something of her life.

I have a daughter too. I can understand the love that parents invest, the hopes and dreams that they carry.

And as peculiar as it probably sounds, I am also thinking about her high-school friendship group and how, in the coming hours, the terrible news will filter through to those young women. I am imagining them poring over her last Facebook or Instagram posts and seeing her grinning back at them. And I make myself hear the roars of their irreconcilable grief.

Yesterday she was alive and she was here.

And now she is gone. An act of inexplicable and abhorrent male violence has stolen everything.

Everything.

~

I do not know what it is like to be a woman and to feel unsafe.

Or to carry my car keys in my fist as I return to an underground carpark or quicken my pace after a jeering catcall outside the pub.

But it is incumbent on me to understand as best I can. And learn more. And be accountable for the way I treat women.

There is a clear non-negotiable responsibility to be a good role model, for my son and his son. And most importantly, a responsibility to be a man who my daughter and her daughter can absolutely trust and rely upon. So too every woman or girl I encounter or pass in the street or in this life.

And if some of you reading this little handbook of whatever it is are fretting over the role you play in family life today or are wondering how you might best counter a directionless retirement ... then let us just practise being our best selves for our family and our friends and for people we don't even know.

Let us be good men.

We need to hold our mates to account, for what they do and what they say.

This gendered violence crisis is a male problem. It is not the problem of a young woman who 'dresses provocatively' or 'was leading me on'. There is no defence that validates 'I couldn't help myself' or 'She had it coming'. There are no excuses for the horrendous violence destroying families. It is perpetrated by men. Men who feel entitled.

And it continues to exist partly because other men look away or pretend that Smithy would surely never do that, because we know he loves his wife and kids.

~

Debra Zanella is the CEO of Ruah Community Services, which offers crucial support for vulnerable and disadvantaged people, including those experiencing homelessness and family and domestic violence. The women who often have nowhere else to go.

I've asked her to cast her experienced eye over my words.

She wants to make it very clear that when I write 'Men who feel entitled', I need to understand it on a deeper level. It's not merely entitlement, she says.

'Geoff, it's men who are unprepared to let go of power. The dominant social construct is the patriarchy. The rise of gender equality and women as economic participants disrupts that system.'

Debra also cautions against pointing to anger as the key component of men's violence against women.

'Anger is something we all experience and is a natural response to situations. Men's violence against women is all about power and the threat of that power being taken away or diminished.'

~

I don't doubt many of you blokes reading this are like me, well intentioned. But I am realising that it's not enough to passively understand male violence. We have to work to stop it.

And we can start by educating our sons and their sons to show respect for women and girls. And to absolutely demand it of them from an early age, because anything less invites disrespect. And disrespect invites aggression.

And calling it 'only a bit of fun' or declaring that 'boys will be boys' is the worst kind of cop-out and an abrogation of our responsibilities.

My phone beeps.

'A twenty-one-year-old man charged with the murder of a young woman has just faced her devastated family in a Ballarat court ...'

~

Rob Andrew is a family-violence counsellor and a man who for many decades has been listening to men confront or occasionally refuse to confront their propensity for violence. Some come to see him under orders from the Family Court, others under orders from the Department of Communities and a few voluntarily because their partners have told them, 'You better bloody get your act together, or I'm gone.'

Rob is eighty-two years of age. Tall and wiry and yes, like Lycra Larry, he is a cyclist too.

He once asked those who attend his workshops to provide a name for it. They settled on 'A group for men who behave badly when they don't get their own way'.

As Debra said, when someone else threatens male power or authority.

Rob doesn't much like phrases like 'male anger' or 'anger management' or 'I have an anger problem' or even that stock phrase 'everyone argues' – because, he says, they offer all-too-easy opportunities for self-justification. And he is blunt about it.

'If you're yelling at your wife and she's not yelling back – is that an argument? No, that's just you being a dickhead.'

He explains further.

'We try to expose the ideas that men have that take them down the path of being disrespectful to women and others. We try to make them take responsibility for what they do. Saying "I was pissed" or "She was giving me the shits" or "I had a bad day at work" are all self-serving justifications that naturalises and normalises the bad behaviour.'

When Rob asks a bloke, 'Why do you do it?' he usually gets not much more than a shrug of the shoulders. So he tells them why they did it.

'You did it because you wanted to, and you could, and you thought you'd get away with it.'

Rob wants accountability.

He tells me about one bloke who attends his workshops because he can barely control his rage when he gets behind the wheel of a car. Other drivers infuriate him, and he validates his often offensive and aggressive behaviour with the simple justification that he 'just can't help it'. Rob says, 'The fella was complaining to me that someone was tailgating him the other night and that yes, he'd hit the brakes hard, yelled at him and given him the finger.'

Rob asked the man if that was helpful, if anything changed because of it. 'No,' came the answer.

'I then asked if there are people in his life who, should they be sitting alongside him, would be uncomfortable hearing those outbursts. He answered immediately, "Yeah, my mum or my kids." So straightaway we are sowing the seeds that this is something he can control. If he is allowed to convince himself he can't help it, he lives by that truth. If he questions that truth, he then has a choice.'

It's true, isn't it?

Him, you, me and us – we have a choice.

~

And it was the disappointment in the eyes of my daughter at the footy that night that led me to change my ways. These days I – usually – just sit at the game and laugh at the madness of others. Disappointed, perhaps, that God clearly hates my team, but resigned to the fact that being a Freo fan is just one of life's challenges that must be endured, hopefully with good grace.

Sport as a microcosm of life.

And frankly, I am better for the realisation.

~

Rob continues.

'The men we meet often believe the world acts against them. That the bad mood they carry home with them after a tough day at work is the reason why the family better watch out tonight.'

Rob wants them to understand it is the discourse they live by that determines how they enter the front door.

'By exposing men to their own processes, they begin to take responsibility for them. So I keep asking them, do you want to keep yelling at your kids? Does your partner want you to keep punching the wall? Do you want the grandkids to be scared of you every time they come over?

'And if that man is serious, in most cases he'll say, "No, not really."

'And then I follow up with, "Does it change anything?"

'And he'll know the answer. "No. It never changes anything."'

~

Look, I know I go hard with this, but without the absolute commitment of you and me and us, it's going to be difficult to make Australian men truly accountable for their violence.

Take this social-media observation from Ian. Yes, another Ian. And his isn't an uncommon opinion.

'If you consume any media at the moment, it looks like all men should just get in the bin. As a man who would rather cut off a leg than hurt a woman, and not knowing any other violent men, surely I can't be the only one who thinks the focus should be on violence in general?'

No, he's not the only one. Ian, like many of us, feels uncomfortable with the finger-pointing and the scrutiny this debate demands. He doesn't think it is fair he is somehow guilty by association.

But I think he is and we are.

So what? Too bad.

If he is a good and non-violent person, then he is particularly well placed to set good examples. To the men and boys he knows. Let them grow up to be like Ian the good and non-violent man, not Ian the excuse-maker.

There are too many of us around.

Chapter 14

Hearing and Listening

I've asked you some daft questions in this book, haven't I?

Well, here comes another one.

Come on, we've got this far.

~

Do you know what you sound like? Not many of us do. Most of us, on hearing our voice recorded and played back, barely recognise it.

'Do I really sound like that? I don't, do I?'

Yes, we do.

After a lifetime of interaction, we probably don't give much thought to how others hear us. How we sound to them. And perhaps even the impact of what we say.

Are we easy on the ear? Is there warmth in our tone? Are we quick to impose our words as statements of intent rather than conversation? Or are they more carefully selected and only delivered when our brain has decided they are right to go?

Who knows. We just say stuff.

So how about a little test of our self-awareness? It's an in-your-head exercise, so no one else will twig as to why you're suddenly looking so engaged in their fascinating company. Conduct a private audit of some of the conversations you have and consciously listen to what you are saying, how you say it and how it is received.

It might be with family. Or your golf mates. Or the woman behind the counter at Myer tomorrow when you go, albeit with great hesitation, to buy yourself a new jumper for winter.

Think about what you will say and how you say it and how someone hears it.

And what conclusions might you draw?

~

(More time-lapse photography of buds opening, flowers blooming, the sun chasing the moon across the sky etc., etc.)

~

How did you go? Was it an interesting exercise? How did it feel being more aware and, because of that, probably more accountable for the impact and value of what you say?

And how were your words received?

~

Maybe it went a bit like this.

It was good you were able to reassure your granddaughter she'll do well in her physics exam. It helped too that you called her the smartest kid in the family.

And clearly there was a non-golfing reason why Clive kept hooking his drive into the trees. He finally revealed he's worried about his dad and how the old man will cope with more radiation treatment. That hand you placed on his shoulder was a comfort. You may have surprised yourself by putting it there.

And then there's Denise, that delightfully cheery woman in Myer who strongly recommended you choose forest green over the boring navy blue. And the sense you had, after talking together, that this empty suburban menswear department was, for her, a place of circumstance rather than choice. Maybe money is tight. Maybe a marriage has ended. Or maybe not; maybe Denise just loves retail.

It was interesting, though, wasn't it?

And I can assure you, life gets a lot more interesting when we are curious about the lives of others. Keep doing the audit. You may hear your voice anew and like it.

At the ABC, I was 'air checked' – audited – every few weeks, by a specialised presentation coach. Every word I uttered on air was placed under forensic scrutiny to ensure I was asking the right questions and allowing room for the answers. It was a sometimes gruesome, confidence-battering experience.

I was quizzed on whether I was actively listening to an interview subject or talkback caller, whether my tone was appropriate or I was allowing myself to become frustrated or annoyed or distracted. I listened to my flubbed interviews and long-winded, self-important questions. I heard myself interrupting others and occasionally focusing on the sound of my own voice rather than listening to theirs.

I did those air checks for sixteen years. I can't say I miss them. Each one felt like a visit to the principal's office. But they were important. They taught me to be accountable for what I say. They taught me about the nuance of language. What people say and how others interpret those words and their intent.

In recent times, I've conducted a few audits to see if I still have some discipline and thoughtfulness about the way in which I communicate with other people. The questions are basic. Be it at the dinner table or in the pub or on the bus.

Was I engaging company? Did I allow others enough space to express their opinions? Did I let them do so without judgement or interruption and correction? Did I ask questions of them and listen attentively to their replies?

Or did I talk over the top of them? And get bored. And stop listening.

I don't write this with any judgement about how you speak or listen to others, but it's an interesting way of assessing how we present to other people. And ascertaining just how much respect or indifference we are showing them.

Have a listen to yourself.

To the sound. To the content. To the delivery. To the response.

~

In this chapter, I want to consider how aware we are of the way we interact. Not just what we say and how we say it, but what we hear and how we listen. I'm not sure we blokes always understand the difference between hearing and listening.

Hearing perceives a sound. It is a passive physiological experience. Listening requires us to absorb the meaning of those sounds. It is an active process. And a voluntary one.

We have to choose to listen.

I wonder if the following scenario is at all familiar?

Partner: 'Don't forget we've got dinner tonight with [insert names here of people whose company you don't like].'

You: 'I didn't know anything about it.'

Partner: 'I told you yesterday.'

You: 'No, you didn't.'

Partner: 'Yes, I did, you just weren't listening.'

The truth is, you might have remembered the dinner date if you were going out with people you really liked. By denying that you were ever told, you're also kind of hoping the subject and the dinner will somehow disappear. And there's just a hint of gaslighting in that.

You are giving your partner pause to doubt whether the conversation took place. It did. And now they are left to manage the fallout.

Scoundrel.

And you probably didn't even notice yourself not listening. You heard only what you wanted to hear. And it wasn't the prospect of breaking bread with [insert names here of people whose company you don't like].

You *were* listening. Selectively.

~

A few years back, a British maker of hearing aids conducted some probably dodgy but amusing research into the idea of selective hearing, and guess what it said about us blokes? The study from Scrivens Hearing Care revealed that we selectively hear things … seven times a week.

And it added up to 388 times a year.

Which didn't add up to me, but the point was brutal.

We don't listen very attentively.

Now there are a couple of other things up for consideration here.

The first is that we may indeed have a hearing problem, and men particularly are notorious for denying that to be a fact. 'I hear perfectly well, thank you, but I wish other people wouldn't mumble so much.' If that sounds like you, you need to act on it.

And the second thing? That same report suggests our partners pretend not to hear what we are saying about 339 times a year. They are nearly as guilty as we are of being indifferent to the conversation of others.

Haha! Knew it!

The consequence of all this?

Apart from the possibility we may all be going deaf ...

Well, if we're not genuinely interested in engaging with others, actively and sincerely, then why would they want to engage with us? Life can get very small and very lonely, very quickly. And isolation kills people.

~

Lindy Burns is a former ABC broadcaster in Melbourne and Newcastle who later became an exceptional mentor and trainer to presenters like me. Lindy is an excellent listener.

Both Lindy and I had careers that required us to be diligent listeners, whether the story was big or small, the conversation important or slight. I remember interviewing Clint Hill, the US Secret Service agent assigned to Jacqueline Kennedy on the day of her husband's assassination, hearing remarkable recollections of his participation in one of the most dramatic moments of 20th-century history ... and then an hour later, I was talking to a listener named Bert, who told me how he copes with the oppressive night-time heat of summer by 'havin' an old damp flannel by me bed and givin' me armpits a bit of a freshen up'.

It was my job to be interested in both stories. And I was.

And the more I practised listening, the better I became. And the more rewarding the conversation.

I ask Lindy how she thinks most of us converse. And her answer surprises me with its bluntness. She reckons we barely do. We just take turns making statements.

'Geoff, in most social circles, we are waiting for the other person to stop talking so we can say our thing. Person 1: "Blah blah blah." Person 2, waits for pause: "Blah blah blah." A lot of people don't even know they're doing it. They think that's the normal way of communicating.'

So, Lindy, how do we become more empathetic listeners?

She begins with a word or two of warning. 'You can't be a better listener if you don't want to be. So, from a purely selfish position, it's useful to understand *why* you want to listen better. What's in it for you? Might it help build better relationships with your family? Get you a better chance of a promotion at work? Learn something new or funny or moving? Realise why something makes you angry or bored?

'Understanding how being a better listener can help you engage and enjoy your life more can be a big incentive to actually do it. Also, in simple terms, being a better listener usually means people like you more. And you get to have a better time with them.'

Lindy has always been someone you want to hang out with for just those reasons. Kind, thoughtful and curious about others.

But there is one more thing she says we blokes need to know: 'You can't be a better listener if you think you're always right.'

I tell her she's thrown an absolute spanner in the works with that.

She will not relent. 'Opening up to and respecting other people's stories and opinions and thoughts usually means that you start to see the world in all of its beautiful complexities. And it reminds us that we are all capable of change and nuance. This brings personal and social enrichment that you would never otherwise experience if you just bang on about your own opinions all the time.'

Essentially, Lindy is saying that if we stop being such bone heads, so entirely fixated on our own opinions and world view, and if we choose to listen closely and are curious and non-judgemental about others, we might have a bloody lovely life.

And it's almost certain that others will say to us, 'You are a very interesting person, [insert own name here], and you look gorgeous in that forest-green jumper.'

~

Now, not all of us blokes want to see the world differently than we already do. Or engage more.

My dad used to flag his unwillingness to do so by simply putting his hand up to his face as if shading his eyes from the sun. It was his protective barrier. It said, 'Don't ask me. Don't.'

And it may seem easier sometimes to retreat into that sullen, silent space. Where we are safe from all that noise and protected from disclosure.

Maggie Dent talked to us about the importance of being willing to share what might trouble us, to speak frankly and to allow ourselves to be vulnerable. Re-read Chapter 11 if you need to. Our partners want us to talk. And they're willing to listen, if we are.

Chapter 15

Learning What the Kids Are Learning Online

Remember the chapter I wrote about you having a good look in the mirror? Did you find it wholesome and life-affirming? Did you go outside and skip through a field of daisies or seek out the VHS box set of *Little House on the Prairie*? Perhaps you flicked through *GQ* magazine looking for the best vegan and cruelty-free facial scrubs, now that you spend more time looking in the bathroom mirror. Such is your new-found determination to smile. To determinedly not be grumpy.

Or you may have just turned away from the mirror and uttered, 'Fuck that.'

You may have suddenly felt the need to watch *Wake in Fright* for a few laughs or sell drugs to primary-school children or kidnap people off the street; anything to get away from the cloying niceness of it all.

What is this 'go and have a look in the mirror and try a big grin' nonsense?

'Life is hard and this prick is talking to me like I'm a bloody [choose your own term]. And I know I'm not allowed to say [choose your own term] anymore, but frankly, I'm getting pretty sick of being told what I can and can't say and what I can and can't think.'

I hope I've got the tenor of that dialogue-in-response about right.

Not everyone sees the world the way I do. Not everyone sees the need for men to have a good hard look at themselves. And not everyone agrees that men should adjust or change anything about who we are. Or even just lighten up a bit.

'Fuck that.'

Indeed, many male commentators, often with huge audiences on legacy-media and now social-media platforms, argue that the world has become increasingly weighted against us. And feminism is to blame! Consequently, there is a need for men to push back against ideas like gender equity or diversity and sneer at wildly successful public figures like Greta Thunberg or Taylor Swift. To reassert our authority. Over all living things.

That's what I want to familiarise you with in this chapter, even if it means you abandon the book and run off to join a white-nationalist organisation and offer up Nazi salutes in public places.

But it is important to acknowledge that there are enormously popular mainstream voices tapping a nerve with disaffected men who are uneasy with changing times. Prominent among these voices is the US podcaster Joe Rogan, who began *The Joe Rogan Experience* podcast back in 2010 and now draws an audience of more than a million listeners daily.

His politics seem libertarian and slightly scattergun. During Covid, he argued that the young and fit had nothing to fear from the virus; he sought to discredit the chief medical officer of the United States, Anthony

Fauci, declaring him 'not a real doctor', and when Rogan finally tested positive, he opted to be treated with the veterinary product ivermectin. He has regularly been damned for promoting conspiracy theories and spreading misinformation.

All of which, in modern America, has made him hugely successful. In late 2024, his three-hour pre-election interview with Donald Trump was credited with winning important new support for the candidate. The following day, Rogan gained 400,000 new YouTube subscribers.

One of his most popular episodes featured a telling observation that 'most men live lives of quiet desperation'. Here's how he explained it at the time: 'I mean, that just terrifies me. It's one of my favourite quotes ever, because it's true. And I've been that guy. You're just in this world where you just can't wait to just run away.'

He is asked, 'And how do people get stuck there?'

He answers, 'Bills and commitment. You have an apartment you have to pay for. You have a car you lease. You have a wife that you have to feed. You have a child you have to raise … And that's where it all comes from.'

To Rogan's credit, he does note that the line comes from the 19th-century American philosopher Henry David Thoreau. Here's the actual quote: 'The mass of men lead lives of quiet desperation. What is called resignation is confirmed desperation. From the desperate city you go into the desperate country and have to console yourself with the bravery of minks and muskrats. A stereotyped but unconscious despair is concealed even under what are called the games and amusements of mankind.'

Now I don't know much about the modern relevance or bravery of minks and muskrats, but essentially he was speaking out about the quiet pain of men who toil long and hard, often in unfulfilling work, and how even though they bust a gut to provide for their families, no one thanks them for it and it leaves them feeling empty and exhausted.

Rogan spoke eloquently about a very real crisis of male confidence. And it resonated hugely. There are, and always have been, lots of men everywhere working their arses off, men who are not sure what it is they are meant to be striving for.

And if more and more of them are feeling undervalued or maligned by the pace of change in the world and the realigning of gender rights and expectations, they are going to feel dispossessed and grumpy. Wondering, perhaps, 'Where the hell do I belong in all this?'

You may well feel the same way.

I wonder, do you?

Interestingly, a generation of listeners now attribute the 'quiet desperation' quote to Rogan directly, because he so successfully articulated their sense of hopelessness.

'You're just in this world where you just can't wait to just run away.'

Why am I citing this as a powerful example? Yesterday I was in the office of an important man with epaulettes on his shirt. I can't name him or the job he does. And taped to the wall behind his desk was a card bearing the phrase 'Living a life of quiet desperation'. When I quizzed him about it, he showed me the Joe Rogan episode on his phone and began to tell me why the quote mattered.

'A couple of months from now, I will be free of that quote. We've already sold the family home and my wife can have everything, as long as she leaves my superannuation alone.' He laughed. 'And then I will finally be free and not' – he pointed to the quote behind his head – 'living a life of quiet desperation any longer.'

Joe Rogan is tapping into the concerns of a weary working man. I respect the sentiment. I bet my dad felt it but could not articulate it.

But did we see the wave of fair opportunity and fair pay and gender equity coming? Did we see how it might impact traditional roles and expectations within our households? The answer is yes. It's been coming for about three generations. If we didn't see it, then we must have been looking the other way.

~

I am going to break it down to its most fundamental. As I understand it, rather than how Joe Rogan might.

Feminism has not made men soft. Men are only being asked to share. Or to move along a bit so someone else can sit down or take their turn on the swing. And I think we can do that with acceptance and grace, without it being a terrible personal slight or a wound to a fragile ego.

~

Joe Rogan's views are increasingly popular among many disaffected men. But of greater concern to me are some other players out there, who advocate for something far more radical and violent. And who want to target your son and grandson.

One of them is a 'success coach' called Andrew Tate – a former champion kickboxer, *Big Brother* contestant and self-proclaimed misogynist. Tate uses every social-media platform that will have him, or not ban him, to openly express his contempt for women – who, he has publicly said, not only 'belong' to men, but should 'bear responsibility' for being sexually assaulted.

At the time of writing, Tate is facing trial in Romania, where he has been charged with rape and human trafficking and forming an organised crime group to sexually exploit women. At the time of writing, Tate has 8.8 million followers on X.

He is handsome, athletic and believes in being at peak fitness to fight the endless fight. I'm just not sure who the fight is with but guess it's anyone his male audience doesn't like.

'It's not safe to be a man anymore,' he tells them.

And on concepts like gender fluidity? 'When someone starts telling you their pronouns, yell "shut the fuck up" and light up a cigar.'

In 2023, *The Guardian* reported that such was Tate's notoriety and fame in British schools, boys were mirroring his misogynistic and aggressive behaviour and were increasingly belittling female classmates and teachers. One putdown, wildly popular in social-media memes, was given in response to any question or request from a woman: 'Shut up and make me a sandwich.'

And the appeal has travelled. Just recently, a schoolteacher acquaintance in Australia told me that she had cautioned a sixteen-year-old male student for his bad behaviour, only to receive the same blank-faced retort: 'Make me a sandwich.'

Which is personally interesting, because one of my earliest lessons in leading an independent life was Mum asking me one day, 'Would you like a sandwich, love?'

To which I replied, 'Yes please, Mum.'

'Well,' she said, 'you know where everything is.'

Andrew Tate and I don't think the same way about the roles, responsibilities and privileges of being a man. But his attitudes do resonate in lots of ways with boys who don't yet know where their head is at, and with older males drawn to the 'manosphere' subculture.

What's that? As far as I understand it, it's a collection of online communities filled with men's rights groups that advocate misogyny, decry feminism and ferment in a kind of male victimhood.

Tate reinforces their views.

On X: 'Females live in a world where absolutely nothing is their fault. They blame everything on everyone else, and when there's a problem they beg a man to fix it. Or cry and scream until a man fixes it. Then once it's fixed they're back to being boss bitches.'

There is a British advocacy group called Hope Not Hate. It assesses Tate's popularity this way: 'His confidence, his money and his lifestyle are all carefully crafted to make his brand of hateful content seem aspirational.'

And it seems to work. In 2023, Hope Not Hate conducted a survey in which it revealed that 80 per cent of boys aged sixteen to seventeen had seen Tate's content. Significantly more of them recognised his photo than that of the then British prime minister, Rishi Sunak.

What's more, 45 per cent of young British men aged sixteen to twenty-four had a positive view of him.

One per cent of girls aged sixteen to seventeen shared that view. One per cent.

If your sons or grandsons follow Andrew Tate and like what he espouses, you might want to know about it. How you choose to respond is your business. But if we have respect for the women and girls in our life, surely we can't ignore a world view that is so toxic?

These views put their safety and wellbeing at risk. These views will cause them to be more scared of men and their motives. And I do not want to shrug my shoulders and look the other way.

Truth is, the manosphere is home to men who spend their thwarted lives wanking into socks and trying to find allies among the young and vulnerable.

~

Then there's this guy. He calls himself the Liver King. He is part of a raw-meat-eating movement in the United States that's based on the belief that we blokes have become soft and enfeebled primarily because we have lost our hunter-gatherer yearnings. The Liver King is the movement's chief meathead, and to be fair, he does appear to have a very, *very* impressive rig.

The Liver King proclaims on his website, 'Our early ancestors understood the sun, the seasons, the beasts, the plants – they were dialled into the rhythms of life and death, the bond, the fight, the feast and famine, and they did it all with an unspoken grace and power lost on the modern manicured man. It's not just tradition, it's baked into our DNA.'

Go and google this modern caveman. He looks well baked.

Unsurprisingly, the Liver King wants us to buy his supplements and do his exercises and, just like those ads in the back of comics in the old days, you too could have a body like his! He claims to have built his vein-popping slab of ab by eating raw liver and beef brains and bull testicles. What has come to light more recently is his appetite for gobbling steroids as the main course. Now he is being sued. Another fraud. Another chancer.

I used to think only Americans were particularly vulnerable to this nonsense, but the internet has invited charlatans like these into the bedrooms of kids everywhere. The smart ones mock him for the doofus he is. And he may well pop an optic nerve and his clogs ten minutes from now.

But some kids believe the Liver King really is the bearer of ancient wisdom. And they too presumably are eating a pound of raw liver every day and looking forward to the day they can hit their womenfolk on the head with clubs. Just like the old days. When men were men.

~

I get in touch again with Maggie Dent to ask how she feels about this. After all, apart from being a professional parenting expert, she has four sons of her own.

'Geoff, I believe the world is full of more good, decent men than the men who promote unhealthy masculinity. I see them everywhere, especially as open-hearted dads who want to be a significant part of Team Parent.

'When men can feel heard and respected in their lives, whether at work or at home, they can feel happier and less grumpy. For that to happen, they need to be willing and able to communicate openly.'

Wondering if you have a role to play mentoring your kids and grandkids? You do.

Be a good role model. Be available to them. Know a bit about their world and their likes and dislikes. Know who seeks to influence their thinking.

And then convince them that Andrew Tate and his ilk are sly, narcissistic douchebags.

Not that the young Swedish climate activist Greta Thunberg seems overly troubled by him.

In December 2022, shortly after his ban from Twitter was lifted, Tate felt the need to taunt her climate concerns by declaring he owned a couple of Ferraris and a quad-turbo Bugatti. He wrote, 'Please provide your email address so I can send a complete list of my car collection and their respective enormous emissions.'

Her reply: 'yes, please do enlighten me. email me at smalldickenergy@getalife.com'.

Chapter 16

Difference

> 'Pretending not to be yourself is one of the most soul-crushing things you can ever do.'
>
> Gemma

You are about to meet Gemma.

She's a twenty-seven-year-old graphic designer and sign maker. Now she is lounging in a chair in the small suburban flat she shares with her partner, Caitlyn, and their dog, Maggie. Gemma is wearing jeans and a black T-shirt and has black polish on her bare toes. She is sipping tea. She's going to talk about an incredible personal journey. And she seems pretty relaxed about it.

I met Gemma a long time ago. She is one of my son Hugh's best friends.

Geoff: 'Gemma, what's your first memory of meeting Hugh?'

Gemma: 'It was in Year Eight, I was walking down one of the outdoor corridors with Indigo. It's really, *really* funny to me to this day, because Hugh was behind us and he just goes, "What are you two, sisters or something?" It's the first thing he ever said to me.'

Geoff: 'Gosh, who'd have known?'

Gemma: 'I know. It's crazy. How did he do it? So yeah, that was the first time we really spoke.'

~

I've asked Gemma to talk to me about her transition from boy to woman. Gemma is a trans woman.

And the reason I asked her to tell her story is that I want you in this chapter to consider the subject of difference. And how you respond to it. Particularly in an era where it has become weaponised – by some politicians, fundamentalist faith groups and cheap opportunists like Andrew Tate.

You might well have a free-spirited, live-and-let-live sensibility, where you have no difficulty seeing all of us, in all our shapes, sizes, dialects or colours as ... well, human beings. Different versions of essentially the same thing.

Or you might not be disposed to see the world that way. Perhaps you draw distinctions and you know what you like and what you don't. What you accept and what you won't. And difference, as it relates to gender, may be a troublesome issue for you.

I want to talk about it, not to throw more fuel on a truly toxic culture-war conversation, but to ask: how would you respond should your sixteen-year-old son or daughter or grandson or granddaughter reveal to you one day that they want to transition? How would you deal with their explanation that they have come to a life-changing determination that they do not feel the body into which they were born reflects the person they are or want to be?

Statistically, it's unlikely to happen.

So why does it matter?

Well, think about it as exercise for our attitudes. An opportunity to stretch our values and beliefs to see how elastic they are.

Indeed, the British philosopher AC Grayling once told me we would all benefit from the occasional airing of our biases and prejudices and willingness to judge others, as if they were washing on a clothesline. To allow the breeze to swirl around them and freshen them up, and we could then decide if they were still relevant or helpful or serving us well.

So, back to the proposition of having gender-fluid kids or grandkids. How might you respond?

To my mind, there are only a couple of choices available to us.

Let's be blunt about it: we can reject them. We can withdraw our love and our support because we feel shame or disgust or because we decide that what they are doing is just wrong. Effectively, however painfully, we can determine they are unworthy of our love.

Or we can tell them that we do love them, and we always will.

Remember, we don't have to like or understand the journey they are on. And that conclusion may not come easily to us. But we can spare this vulnerable and under-attack cohort further pain. And whatever happens next, they will know that someone in the family has their back.

I think the options are as fundamental as that.

And in case you read a lot of right-wing media, let me be clear: the numbers we speak of are very small. So, for most of us, this is purely hypothetical. Recent estimates from the Murdoch Children's Research Institute suggest that the prevalence of young people identifying as trans is about one in 100 in the Western world. About 45,000 schoolchildren in Australia, or about 1.2 per cent, are thought to identify as trans.

But it might be your grandkid. Or maybe your thirty-five-year-old son who doesn't want to present to the world as a man anymore. So hear me out.

Our sex is determined at birth, but gender, as noted by the World Health Organization, is a social construction of how we look, act and express who we are and what we identify with.

Just as femininity and masculinity are constructs. Or why we assume girls play with Barbie dolls or boys with Tonka trucks.

And gender is a broad spectrum of types, some of which you might never have heard of, let alone comprehend: transgender, gender fluid, non-binary, cisgender, gender neutral, pangender ... The list is growing as more people explore their sense of self.

Gender is not a binary between man and woman. Although you or your faith might see it only in those terms.

Just for the record, I identify with the gender I was assigned to at birth, and that makes me cisgender.

Just in case someone asks. Which they never will.

You've probably heard about pronouns too – where 'he' and 'she' have been joined and sometimes replaced by 'they' and 'them'. It sounds weird, and I know some of you reject the premise utterly. And that's entirely your business.

But I reckon you should meet Gemma anyway, because she's a bloody great person. And there is always value in saying hello to someone you don't know.

~

The story so far.

When Gemma went to high school, she was relieved to be free of the name-calling and bullying she'd experienced in the primary-school playground. By the time she entered this new world, with so many kids she'd never met before, she had decided to lay out some ground rules.

Gemma: 'If anyone tried to bully me in high school, I made a very big point of threatening them with physical violence if they ever did it again, and it worked really well. There were so many of these little troublemakers that would try and start shit, basically. They would think that they were so hard and so cool, and then I would just mop the floor with them.'

Geoff: 'So I remember you as this kid who would skateboard across Perth to get to our place. What was going on with the old Gemma?'

Gemma: 'It's a story that feels very long to me, especially when I went back and traced it when I was twenty, which is when I started transitioning. I remember when I was fourteen, I stayed up late watching a BBC documentary. It was about trans people in Britain, and I didn't know anything about it. I remembered looking at it and being like, "Oh, what even is that?" I watched this whole documentary, which was six episodes. I think I watched it two or three times. And then I realised how often I had obsessive thoughts about lots of girls at high school who I didn't even really like, but I had a feeling that, "I wish I could be like them."'

Excited and terrified by what she was discovering, Gemma did what so many do and nailed down the lid of her feelings. It was too dangerous to consider and too hard to process. And she certainly couldn't share it with anyone.

Definitely not her parents.

Over the next few years, she struggled. She slept poorly and at one point was at serious risk of self-harm. She saw a psychiatrist and was treated for depression and anxiety. A low-dose antidepressant helped her sleep better, and she went to university to study graphic design.

And one day, something happened.

Gemma: 'I was in a good mood. It was a nice day. I was well fed, and I'd been learning and I just felt really good. But at the same time, I felt this void in my chest, and I realised I'd always felt it, but I didn't know what it was. Then this girl walked past me, and she had this really cute skirt on, and I was like, "I wish I could look like that." Then I was like, "Whoa, whoa, whoa, whoa, whoa! What was that?"'

Gemma all but springs from her chair with the retelling. She is laughing hard. But back then, she spent the next fortnight trying to work out what she had just revealed to herself and what to do next. She decided to tell her friend Katya.

Gemma: 'We went to the Rosemount and we had a pint. I was like, "Here's the thing. Look, I'm trans, I just am. I figured this out about myself, and you are the first person I wanted to talk to about it. Because I'm a little nervous about what to do next."

'But I realised that void in myself, as soon as I started to process and understand myself, it both dissipated and expanded to fill my entire body. Pretending not to be yourself is one of the most soul-crushing things you can ever do. I think I realised that's what had caused me to feel the way that I had been feeling.

'So I said, "I think I would rather be dead than not go through with this, so fuck, I guess we're doing it." And then we went to the shops, and she helped me buy my first bra and stuff like that, which was really cute.

Obviously, I didn't need one at the time, but I wore it all the time. It's hard to explain how affirming that was for me.'

~

I sense Gemma is telling me this story from the safety of now. She is able to look back and recognise her resilience. Of which she needed buckets.

~

Today, Gemma is seven years into hormone-replacement therapy that has significantly dampened her testosterone levels, fed her body oestrogen and softened her look. So what's that like?

Gemma: 'The thing that a lot of people miss is that when you start taking hormone-replacement therapy, your brain feels different, because you have different hormones in there. That was one of my greatest feelings of euphoria actually – the difference in the way that my cognition worked. I really, really liked that. It was hard at first because, basically, it's like a new puberty. So it takes about three years for all of the changes to be done.'

Geoff: 'What is different? What feels different?'

Gemma: 'God, it's so hard to explain. I think a good example is that I often found that when I was distressed before, I would get angry easily or irritated easily. But now, if I'm finding myself really distressed, I will cry or something like that. It feels like the right response to have. I always used to feel very disconnected from my mind and how it should have worked and my body and how it should have worked, whereas now everything makes a lot more sense to me. I feel like these are my genuine reactions to things, if that makes sense.'

Geoff: 'I'm about to offer up one of my favourite questions. Okay?'

Gemma: 'Okay.'

Geoff: 'Who do you see when you look in the mirror?'

Gemma: 'I see myself. I think I look back at photos of myself from when I was nineteen, and I don't even know who that is. The eyes are the same, I guess, but ... It's like we're the same person, obviously, but that was never me. I was in that body, but that was never me.'

I wonder what her parents see in Gemma today? Suffice it to say the relationship has been fraught, and neither of us wants to push the issue too hard. Or embarrass or punish or express regret. But ... there have been some encouraging signs.

Gemma: 'In the past couple of years, both of them have said to me, multiple times, that, "Even though I still find this hard, something that makes it easier for me is seeing how happy it makes you." I think that's the thing that you keep in mind, really. Yeah, this is really new for a lot of people.'

Geoff: 'What do you think men of your father's generation and my generation need to understand better about your journey or the journey of any trans person?'

Gemma: 'I think that it can be easy to get mired down in the idea that you need to understand all these aspects of the trans experience. That you need to understand what it feels like to be on replacement therapy or what it feels like to have gender dysphoria or euphoria or whatever. But it isn't what you need to understand, because those are things that will, in many ways, always be alien, and that's okay. There's stuff about men of that age group that I will find alien, but that doesn't mean it's bad. It's just not my lived experience.

'I think the main thing you need to understand is this is a person. The main thing to take away from trans people isn't that they're this terrifying force who want to change everybody and cause great disruption and everything. Most people just want to be happy.'

And with that statement of the beautifully obvious, Gemma shrugs her shoulders and smiles at me.

Yet the truth is trans people in Australia are dealing with escalating levels of harassment and violence. And I cannot reconcile how, in a world with so many conflicts and problems, some political figures and their media acolytes would choose to conflate gender issues the way they do, determinedly trying to run trans people out of town to win the cheers of a baying mob. Prioritising the alienation and rejection of a very small group of vulnerable people who only want to be recognised for who they are.

So let's focus on Gemma and you and me. What would she like you to consider if your kids or grandkids come to similar realisations as she has?

'The main thing to think about is: how can I get to know this person and see them for who they are? Because then they can do the same thing for you. I think that's what it's about.

'I think there's a lot of tribalism these days. There's a lot of identity politics, which I really hate as a word anyway, but I think people too easily are jumping to these extremes. I think social media makes it worse. I think that at the end of the day, it's important to try and sit down and think about people as people.

'You work with a lot of people. You don't like every single one of them, but you can respect them as a person, and there's stuff about everybody that you can see as being good. So if Janice in HR can get it, then I don't see why nobody else can.'

Gemma pauses. Offers another smile and sips her tea.

We say our farewells, and as I close the gate behind me, I repeat to myself, 'If Janice in HR can get it, I'm sure the rest of us can.'

Gemma and Caitlyn plan on getting married next year.

~

The challenges ahead for Gemma and those who identify differently to me and possibly you are going to be enormous. In the United States, particularly since the start of Donald Trump's second term as president, lawmakers in many states are pushing to introduce legislative change that will limit the access of trans people to healthcare, military service, the opportunity to play sport and even the use of bathrooms.

What is apparent is that trans people are fighting for their human rights to be acknowledged and for sex discrimination laws to recognise gender discrimination too.

They may or may not succeed.

And while most of us can surely agree that the search for identity, for a place in this world where we truly belong, is a universal idea, there is also the hard truth that there has always been a price to be paid for difference.

I'd really prefer our kids and grandkids not to have to pay that price.

And certainly not for political expedience.

And just to give you an even greater sense of the ludicrous explosion of media stories that are helping to light fires of anger and resentment against people like Gemma. And fitting a mad narrative that is patently untrue ...

In November 2023, the BBC reported that a school in Wales was forced to deny rumours that had spread online that it was providing cat litter trays ... for students who identified as cats. So voracious were those rumours, the school had to write to parents to say there was no special treatment for 'pupils who might identify as an animal of any kind'.

There were no cat litter trays.

Because none of the kids identified as cats.

Stories like that might make some of us laugh. But these days there are enough people who want to believe anything that endorses a prejudice. Such stories are mischievous misinformation, written to create outrage and to stoke anger – and put members of the trans community at risk.

Can you imagine if your kids or grandkids became targets of that hate?

Enough said.

Chapter 17

Crisis, What Crisis?

Please don't eat raw bull testicles. The subject has been on my mind.

True, I have seen some pet-food suppliers declare them a great source of high-quality protein, and apparently they deliver a wide range of B-group vitamins ... But they are pet food.

And yes, in the spirit of transparent research, I also went on a US site called Frankie's Free Range Meats, and admittedly his human customers do eat them and confidently endorse their testosterone-raising qualities. Ryan, for example, declared a surge in his vitality. 'They taste similar to oysters. I eat them frozen and raw.' Ryan may well be living his best life with a hot new babe. Good for you, Ryan.

Or he might be sitting in a tiny fleapit of an apartment trying to hide his seemingly permanent stiffy from his ever-curious staffy. Is Ryan doing okay? Is Ryan a happy and well-adjusted man?

All of which returns me to the question I pondered at the very start of this book. Are we 21st-century men in crisis? You know, an actual crisis?

Do you think we are?

Do you think you are?

~

Do you ever consider the question? Perhaps not.

We men have been blessed and cursed with the enormous capacity to simply not think deeply about intensely personal issues or our profound inner selves, if we don't want to. And we usually don't want to.

Instead, we favour the pragmatic approach and go and wash the car, or head to Bunnings to find a replacement downlight for the one that keeps blinking and fizzing in the kitchen. Better to be useful. That way, we believe, we are sending at least some kind of unspoken message to our family that says, look, I'd love to be more available to talk with you, my teenage daughter, about that TikTok video that's doing the rounds that is *so* embarrassing – but as you can see, I am rather busy. Fixing things. Solving problems of a different kind.

And, admittedly, not understanding much about your weird hormonal young life.

Do know that I'd love to be a more evolved, sensitive and intuitive father, but somehow that talent has been buried so deep in my hippocampus, I simply can't access it easily today. I simply can't quite manage to sit at the end of your bed and just listen to you speak.

Uninterrupted.

Or without wondering if your windowsill could do with a coat of paint.

By the way, how many of you blokes have already considered whether a hippocampus is a boarding school for giant wading mammals? Our natural dad-joke instincts may yet prove invaluable during this potentially disquieting appraisal of self.

So, yes, there are lots of important discussions taking place to determine why we blokes might be feeling a bit shaky these days. We've already touched on a fundamentalist view, that we have lost much of our hunter-gatherer, poo-flinging identity because we don't go out and kill mammoths and drag them back to the campfire anymore.

But I would also counter that modern manly incarnations have compensated quite nicely with a hickory-smoked brisket cooked on a slow barbecue. And apparently hundreds of thousands of Australian blokes are now members of BBQ-linked social-media communities and often gather by the smoker for twelve hours to talk about short ribs and pickles ...

And, if we're lucky, their 'feelings'.

Admittedly, it doesn't quite compare to the kill-or-be-killed thrill of man-on-mammoth action, but it still sounds like a pretty high-protein blokey interaction to me.

Well done, those men. Even if they prefer medium rare.

~

Okay, so we're not hunter-gatherers anymore. Not really. What about our famous and fabulous brute strength? Our innate ability to lift heavy things?

Well, let's be frank, who really cares?

No one, apart from Helmut over the road, plays the piano much anymore, so there is almost no need to carry one up two flights of stairs. And it's been a long while since a kid was trapped under the back wheel of a car.

Truth is, our bulging biceps have largely been supplanted by technological might and artificial intelligence that lifts and organises and distributes life in a way we can barely recognise. Our wharves, once home to jutting-jawed men with massive tattoos and deeply belligerent attitudes to authority, now rely on cranes, straddle carriers and reach stackers to bring you your new double-cab ute. The ship that brought it to our shores is steered by a tiny joystick. And in an Amazon-era warehouse, there are barely any humans at all: a robot has already sorted your order and attached it to a drone, and it should be whirring above the front porch of your place within a few minutes.

The ability to hunt and lift heavy things. A talent that was uniquely ours as men. Not in such demand as it once was.

And apparently it wasn't that unique anyway. New research suggests that prehistoric women frequently went hunting and were physiologically well suited to it. We might have swung our clubs with greater gusto, but they apparently had the superior endurance to run down a fleeing beast. Nine thousand years on, and remains of those women have just been discovered in Peru with hunting weapons by their side.

That'd be right.

And while we're at it, just a note about mammoths.

I've been reading that Australian scientists have recently been messing about in the kitchen with the DNA sequence for a mammoth protein that they have stuffed into the stem cells of sheep, producing ... 21st-century mammoth meat. No one's eaten it yet, because it's been a few thousand years since we've tasted such a protein and it could play merry hell with our guts.

But the fact is, the modern-day version of primitive us could soon put mammoth meat back on the menu. Barbecued in backyard barrel-drum smokers across the land.

The conclusion? We don't hunt and we don't lift heavy things anymore presumably because we appear to have evolved to the point where life no longer requires us to do so.

That's okay, isn't it? Crisis averted?

Well, hang on a bit.

~

What about our relationship with the girls? The Wilma Flintstones and the Betty Rubbles who picked ticks out of Fred and Barney's hair and kept them warm at night. Nothing's changed there, has it?

Well, it might be best to yabba dabba don't go there. The news is not so good.

We've already talked quite a lot about our partners in this book. I hope you heard the air-raid sirens. And I hope you've twigged by now that those relationships may well be on borrowed time. Not only are women historically well equipped to hunt and gather, but increasingly we're told they are getting a bit fed up with us. And as I've previously pointed out, the statistics suggest more and more of them are wanting to explore the possibility of life without us in it.

Maggie Dent reckons far too many wives and mums have been held captive by the unpaid responsibility of running a household, raising children and dealing with the male head cold. And they are increasingly asking, 'Is that all there is?'

And they are finding out the answer: 'No, it doesn't have to be.'

Maggie tells me, barely able to conceal her glee, 'Once we're past menopause and the need to feed the kids, more and more of us will be off!'

Off? I'm sensing she means somewhere other than book club.

She means finding new lives. Becoming Peruvian hunters or amateur vulcanologists or learning Cantonese or firing the burner on a hot-air balloon and embarking on adventures that may or may not include you. Or me.

~

Now, much as I like dropping these doomsday scenarios into your lap, just to make sure you're not dozing off – let's get a more sophisticated take from one of Australia's foremost academics in this space, Professor Michael Flood at the Queensland University of Technology. He has published widely on topics including violence prevention, men and masculinity, gender equality, men's advocacy, fathering and pornography. He is the father of two kids, and on the Friday afternoon we Zoom-meet, he is responsible for another couple of terrors and has to leave the room repeatedly to help with sandwich preparation and kitchen chaos.

First up, Professor, on behalf of men everywhere, are we in the greatest crisis of our lives? Are we being scrutinised like never before?

'No,' says Professor Flood.

I'll let that sit there for a moment before he explains more.

'There are clearly some men who are in crisis. Men who feel like they've had the rug pulled out from under them. Men being made to reassess how they should behave in households, and how they should treat their wives. And, you know, some men are reeling. Some men are struggling with shifts in the kind of material circumstances of men's and women's lives and shifts in gender expectations.

'But I think other men are thriving. Other men are relishing the opportunities they now have, to take time off work and spend time with their young children.

'And there's far greater social acceptance today of the fact other men can finally hold hands with their male partners walking down the street or get married to them.'

Thanks, Prof. So some of us are struggling, some are thriving. And frankly, I am encouraged that in 21st-century Australia, men and boys may not have to wear the one-size-fits-all uniform of male expectation. Our sons and their sons might indeed have the opportunity to lead less prescribed lives.

They've been offered an invitation to step out of what, for many, is an ill-fitting stereotype. Of stoicism and silence. And repressed emotions. And perhaps to be given the opportunity to explore and find a more authentic self. To wear what they want and be who they want.

And that would look good on any of us, at any age.

But what of those men who Professor Flood says are reeling? Unsure of the roles they are meant to play in changing times and unlikely to loosen the shirt-and-tie combo.

I wonder if you are one of them.

Do you feel the rules have changed and perhaps the ground beneath you is shifting? And while I don't know your circumstances, is it a pretty safe assumption that, for whatever reason, you don't feel very secure? And perhaps you are not being listened to as you once were? And fewer of those around you are deferring to your judgement and opinion? Or relying on you?

And if you are nodding vigorously or muttering, 'Fucking oath,' then I'm guessing that is a pretty unsettling place to sit right now.

I'm just guessing. And thank you for considering these endless suggestions.

Please keep reading. None of this is scary. Let it represent an opportunity with which you may choose to engage.

But how do we engage, or buy in, when we don't really understand some of the arguments?

Professor Flood, what is masculinity anyway? And why has it been weaponised with the word 'toxic' attached to it?

'Geoff, let me start with the word itself. For me, masculinity refers to the social and behavioural expectations placed on men and boys. What it looks like varies across cultures, varies over history and can be both good and bad. It's kind of an open-ended definition of what is expected of blokes.

'Toxic masculinity refers to one version of those expectations. A version that is limiting or damaging for the men and boys who try to live up to it and is also harmful or damaging for those around them. So when people talk about toxic masculinity, or at least when advocates and informed commentators talk about it, they are typically talking about the expectations that men must be rigidly heterosexual, their need to be tough, to be stoic, to be in control and to not express doubts or anxiety.

'And when they [men who are under these expectations] respond to challenges, they do so often with violence.'

I plough in here and ask, what is the cost of all that – to us and all those around us?

Professor Flood explains, 'There is a wealth of evidence that the men who try to conform to that model of masculinity pay a significant cost. A cost in terms of their physical health, their emotional health, in terms of their connections with others, in relationships and friendships and so on. They're literally more likely to contemplate suicide and to attempt suicide than other men.

'So conformity to that model of masculinity, what some people call toxic or others called traditional or stereotypical masculinity, is harmful for those men. Particularly conformity to the elements to do with stoicism, to never expressing weakness.'

I understand.

But crikey, that's bleak, isn't it? A rigid and unyielding existence. A life where any doubt or anxiety or vulnerability is to be feared and rejected and hidden from light. And the opportunity to be one's true self is vigorously and emphatically denied.

And we've repeated that pattern. Generation after generation.

I can't believe how weird and sad that is.

And, of course, implicit in that toxic masculinity, beyond the sorrow-filled fear of who we might otherwise be, is our extraordinarily destructive ability to hurt others.

Professor Flood continues: 'Yeah, toxic masculinity is also implicated in men's mistreatment of others, implicated in men's violence against other men, implicated in men's domestic and sexual violence against women, implicated in men's non-involvement in parenting, their lack of involvement in fatherhood.'

So everyone loses.

~

Let me, at this important moment, acknowledge those of you for whom this toxicity is just a grotesque curiosity found in other men. It is not the story of most of us.

Not all men are emotionally barren and unfeeling. Not all men are rapists and killers. We are not all inherently dangerous or misogynistic. But we can be.

And unless we learn to accept some of the ugly truths and call them out and actively work to undo them – then we are complicit. We are in the same room, we are seeing what is happening, but too many of us are doing nothing.

~

So let me have another crack at an idea I put to you in the chapter about anger.

How accountable are you prepared to be, to help end this scourge? Will we, that's you and me, call out male violence in its many forms? Physical assault ... coercive control of a partner ... would we, you and me, step in, if we witnessed it? Could another person be assured that if they came to us in need of help, we would be willing and able to provide it?

And even more fundamental perhaps, are those women and girls safe in our company?

I believe the answer, broadly, is yes. I can even hear you say it. But I want us to say it louder and mean it and be ready to act on it.

I do wonder how you're absorbing this. I wonder what my dad would have said about it. He'd recognise it, I think. Accept some of the truths in it. But he probably wouldn't engage further. He certainly wouldn't consider questions about a toxicity within or about the opportunity to seek a more authentic self. Or consider talking openly if something was bothering him.

It would sound indulgent. Perhaps even embarrassing. He would go and water the tomatoes.

And yet I do know that my dad wanted me to be a good man and have a better life than he did. Most parents do.

I remember coming home for a visit, back in the mid-1990s. I'm married with a daughter now, and he and I are having a beer on the back veranda. We're pleased to see each other. He takes a sip and then says, 'Show me your hands.'

I offer them. He turns them over and looks at me with a smile and declares, with affection and not a hint of accusation, 'Not a callus there, my boy.'

'Only from all the typing,' I reply. Proudly.

His hands had done hard physical labour all his life. The heavy lifting of a certain kind of male expectation. I knew he was pleased that I wasn't spending my working life digging ditches and trenches and leach drains, as he so often had. He was proud too.

When my son, Hugh, was about eight, I remember asking him, perhaps with a similar kind of gentle, teasing curiosity, 'Have you ever peeled an orange in your life? Do you even know how?'

'No,' he said and continued to busy himself with his Game Boy.

I imagine one day soon he will ask, with similar good humour, 'Dad, do you even know how to illegally download a streaming service using a VPN?' And I will say 'No' and have to admit I barely understand the question.

We are all similar and different. For better or worse. Evolved in some ways, but still learning. And I am comfortable with that. The scrutiny and a growing demand for greater accountability. I do not see it as a threat to who I am. I am not being targeted or blamed.

And neither are you. Unless you have such a thin skin you hear new voices and contrary opinions only as a personal affront.

Let's see it as an invitation to learn new stuff. To probably mess up on occasion, but to explore something different and, I think, better. Fairer for others. It is an opportunity. And we lose nothing from it.

~

I have been the recipient of great privilege in this life. Maybe you have too. So before I let Professor Flood go, I want to talk to him about the phrase 'white male privilege'. It too is being spat at us, and many of us are taking offence.

What? Me? Male privilege?

Professor Flood says, 'Geoff, I think this is the one issue that many men push back on. So many men, in fact, offer broad support for gender-equality issues. They think that of course women and men should have the same rights and responsibilities. And of course women shouldn't be subjected to discrimination or prejudice or harassment. But many men will bristle at the idea that they themselves may have benefited from those systemic inequalities.

'And you know, I'm a professor, a senior academic, and it's easy to think that my achievements and my CV is simply the result of my own efforts, my own skill. But there have been other factors at play. I think, for example, for men who are CEOs and board members or managers, the fact that they're typically hired by other people who look just the same as them, or went to the same private school as them, is a significant advantage.

'There are various kinds of unearnt privilege that we receive, and when I open my mouth in a meeting, I'm probably going to be listened to more readily than if a woman sitting next to me says exactly the same thing.'

There's some blunt truth-telling right there. Women know it. We pretend not to.

I remember the first time I became truly aware of the phrase 'white male privilege'. It arrived in a text from a listener accusing me of gender-based assumptions in some remark I'd made. I pushed it away defensively rather than consider what it meant. In my head, I told myself – as Professor Flood just told me – that I'd worked bloody hard for any success I enjoyed. That I was a fair-minded bloke, well aware of gender imbalance and keenly of the view it must be corrected.

Fortunately for me, I also had a daughter in her twenties, who I knew would tear my brittle and defensive argument to pieces with hard facts about gender discrimination and pay disparity and the glass ceiling in the corporate world and yes, Dad, the uncanny ability of blokes to fail *upward*. So I sat on the idea for a while.

And I want you to consider doing the same thing.

Let's just sometimes stop pulling the reflex pin of the outrage grenade. I promise it won't blow up in our faces.

I realised – eventually – that I responded the way I did because the observation was framed as an accusation and I became defensive. People do. But when I looked at it with space and a genuine willingness to be reflective, I concluded that of course I have been the beneficiary of this privilege. It's a membership of a club that has such obvious advantages, I don't even have to sign up. I don't even need to be made aware of the conditions, because for me and you, there are none.

The Boys' Club.

Welcome.

How can we help?

Spend a moment imagining what it is to be a woman who has ascended to the pinnacle of a previously male-dominated profession. She might be a prime minister, or a CEO, or a sports presenter. The truth is, whether it's loudly expressed to her or just an ever-present undercurrent of unspoken bias, she knows she will have to be twice as good at her job to find acceptance. Twice as good.

Professor Flood again: 'It's uncomfortable to be told that you're a member of a privileged group, a group that has received some unfair forms of advantage. Or even more confronting to be told that you're perpetuating the problem. And I'm glad to see that, for example, there's growing attention to the idea of calling men in, rather than calling men out.'

I interrupt here. 'Calling men in?'

'Well, calling men out is a part of what we describe as cancel culture. There is a kind of self-righteous, puritanical, shame-inducing way of calling men out on sexism or on poor behaviour. And I think there are better ways. There are more compassionate ways, that are more sensitive ways to bring men into those conversations. We do have to address the serious problems of sexism and violence and of inequality, but I think we can do so in compassionate and constructive ways.'

Professor Michael Flood wants us to be a welcome part of a discussion rather than an enemy. Could you do that? Be prepared to let your guard down enough to listen, maybe concede the point and not be undone because of it?

It's worth a try. Because sometimes the light-bulb moment arrives. And then we might be more inclined to listen to the next thing someone else says, rather than close down.

At this juncture, the tail of a cat walked across our Zoom meeting and temporarily muted the conversation. After which, the Professor had to go and attend to his kids in the kitchen.

But I take comfort from his words and I hope you do too. When we feel under attack, when we are defensive about all this, we lose our ability to remain engaged and curious about the changes occurring in our world.

I think we can choose to see it one of two ways – an assault on us, or an exercise in personal growth.

May I at this point acknowledge that you probably don't like reading sentences that use phrases like 'exercise in personal growth'? And I will try hard to avoid them. But even the most grumpy and cynical and mean-spirited among us know there is no going back. And I do think it is important for us to understand that the behaviours others find repellent about the toxic aspects of our masculinity – they're still occurring.

Every day. Everywhere.

And there's one coming up. It's all about an unwanted kiss.

Chapter 17 and a Bit

A Career-Ending Kiss

It is the evening of 20 August 2023, and the Spanish women's football team has just won the World Cup with a one–nil victory over England in Sydney. During the presentation ceremony, forward Jenni Hermoso is embraced and then kissed by Luis Rubiales, president of the Royal Spanish Football Federation.

He is clearly delighted. She is not. A worldwide television audience of about 1.5 billion people watch it. Six weeks later, that kiss will lead to his resignation, create a furore in football and in Spain itself and completely overshadow the extraordinary performance of Jenni and her team.

Why does the retelling matter here? Because that kiss arrived some six years after the explosion of the #MeToo movement following the arrest and later conviction of the Hollywood film producer Harvey Weinstein on sexual assault and rape charges. #MeToo has become a formidable symbol of empowerment and action against generations of men who have harassed and assaulted women without being held to account.

Men. Who harass and assault women.

Perhaps not blokes like you and me. Perhaps blokes just like you and me.

And so the moment Luis Rubiales hugged Jenni Hermoso, put his hands behind her head to draw her closer and then kissed her full on the mouth, that audience of billions began to discuss whether he was entitled to do so, whether it was inappropriate to do so or, worse, whether he'd committed an act of sexual coercion and abuse. For some men, it was 'just a kiss'; Rubiales called it 'just a little peck'. They argued he was simply excited that Spain's team had just won the biggest prize in all of women's football. It was just a kiss.

Hermoso said it was uninvited and non-consensual.

What also matters here is context. What had led up to this match, this moment?

~

The Guardian, Friday 8 September 2023: 'The uproar over Rubiales' behaviour as well as the applause and standing ovation given to him by members of the federation after he railed against "false feminism" shone a spotlight on the deep sexism that continued to exist in some Spanish institutions ...'

The story explained how, months earlier, fifteen members of the national team refused to play for coach Jorge Vilda. All accused him of bullying and harassment. The Spanish Federation, led by Rubiales, demanded they 'admit their error and apologise' or they would never play again. Indeed only three of the fifteen squad members ended up playing in the World Cup.

How extraordinary, then, after having been subject to poor pay and a culture of fear and bigotry and sexism, that they still won. How sad, though, that their triumph was tainted by a man and a football federation who played so little part in that success. Triumph seems to have come not because of the federation but despite it.

The ABC journalist and commentator Annabel Crabb put it this way: 'Women watching the broadcast recoiled. For several weeks, we'd watched powerful women be great at their jobs on TV.

'And now we were watching this glorious sportswoman reduced to an object, a body to be grabbed and snogged against her will. By her boss. In front of a giant global audience.'

~

So, fellas, in case we were wondering, that was why it wasn't received as just a kiss or a clumsy moment. It was received as an insult to women, and it came from a man who felt entitled to do what he wanted.

And perhaps that's why we keep hearing other people talk about 'toxic masculinity' and the 'crushing patriarchy'. It's a protest against male privilege and entitlement. And today this entitlement is being called out as unacceptable behaviour. The consequence of which is that our sons or perhaps grandsons will now be taught about consent at school, about what consent means.

Indeed, I've just read that in my home state of Western Australia more than 1100 schools have committed to include more lessons to equip children with skills to develop safe relationships, avoid harmful situations and help prevent them becoming perpetrators of sexual violence. Education Minister Tony Buti declared, 'Stronger education is needed to promote a culture of respect and help prevent all forms of harassment and assault, including family and domestic violence.'

That, surely, is a good idea. Educate.

Meanwhile, in Spain, beyond the football pitch, in offices and workplaces across the country, women are speaking up with greater confidence about the sexism that has made their lives miserable. Their cry? *Se acabó*. Which means, 'It's over.'

In October 2023, Luis Rubiales was banned by FIFA for three years from having any involvement in football, after being found guilty of 'offensive behaviour and violations of the principles of fair play'. In February 2025, the high court of Madrid found Rubiales guilty of sexual assault and ordered him to pay a fine of €10,000 and stay away from Hermoso for twelve months.

~

It's Sunday morning. And I am sitting with my wife and some female friends, having coffee. I tell them I want to include the resignation of Luis Rubiales in this book, as an example of how men's misbehaviour, once indulged or ignored, is now being scrutinised. And why we blokes better wise up to that fact, accept it, understand it and own it.

I then sat back and said nothing, as the women around me reflected on that 'kiss' and its aftermath. There was a great chorus of agreement and anger.

One woman, a high-school teacher, now nearing her own retirement, looked at her friends and declared, 'And there is not one woman here who hasn't been subjected to that unwanted kiss, that presumptuous touching or that complete invasion of space. Not one.'

And they all concurred.

And I sat quietly and didn't know what to say. And that was alright.

Chapter 18

What Makes a Life Worth Living?

How are you feeling? You know, coming off the back of some, let's be honest, slightly challenging academic analysis by Professor Flood and a small lecture about keeping your lips to yourself if you ever get to present a trophy to a Spanish football star. Are you happy to press on, or would you prefer to go to the dentist or munch on a bull's testicle?

I'm banking on the fact you are still engaged. Perhaps even curious to know why we increasingly hear that sharp accusation of being pale, stale and male. Why are we being called that? I need some context. I need to know if we're copping a fair whack or a cruel one. And when I need perspective, there is one man to whom I like to turn.

I have interviewed the psychologist and social researcher Hugh Mackay many times. Hugh is a bestselling author of twenty-four books and has for more than half a century been talking to Australians of all ages and backgrounds, to ascertain who we are and what matters to us. Taking our temperature. Hugh is eighty-six years of age. He knows us pretty well. And he knew our dads too.

Anyway, Hugh wrote a book a few years ago called *The Good Life: What Makes a Life Worth Living?* And he drew this conclusion:

> The greatest monument to any of our lives will not be in stone, but in the living legacy – the influence we have had on other people at every point of connection with the human family. You don't have to be rich to leave a positive legacy; you don't have to be intelligent, famous, powerful or even particularly well organised, let alone happy. You need only to treat people with kindness, compassion and respect, knowing they will have been enriched by their encounters with you.

Hugh has long advocated that the best way to deal with the onset of negativity and cynicism and distrust is to engage with and to care about others.

Hugh, it's always a pleasure to speak with you. I was thinking the other day that we wouldn't have dared called my dad's generation of men 'pale, stale and male', but it is a familiar catchcry today. Why is it being uttered?

'Geoff, this is the latest manifestation of the long-overdue gender revolution. It's a feminist backlash against the male-supremacist culture that held sway for thousands of years.'

Hugh is keen to get to the point.

'It's a shock to older men because they know their fathers and grandfathers would never have had to cop such a label. But it's a short-term price being paid by older men for their perceived membership of the blokes' club that, for aeons, either ruled the roost or thought it did. Male supremacism, like white supremacism, is an ugly stain on our long cultural history, and many blokes, especially younger ones today, won't have a bar of it. The thing is, older blokes are paying the price for having been too slow to embrace the meaning of gender equality.'

I ask Hugh if he thinks our current state of grumpiness is peaking, or whether we have always been predisposed to the harrumph as we get older.

'Historically, many – but by no means all – older men have tended towards grumpiness for two main reasons. The first relates to their work life. It was Gareth Evans, the former Australian foreign minister, who coined the phrase "relevance deprivation syndrome", based on the huge but understandable mistake of men using their job as a major source of their personal identity.

'It's hard to let go of "I'm an architect, broadcaster, politician or plumber", if your sense of who you are has been primarily determined by your job. Culturally, that tendency was strongly reinforced by the pre-gender-revolution idea that the man was the breadwinner and head of the house and that his main role in life was to work, to earn, to provide – while his wife's main role was nurturing and housekeeping. It was dangerous for men [to let go] back then, because of the "relevance deprivation" trap that lay in wait for them, but now, in the light of the gender revolution, it's crazy stuff.

'Secondly, and I understand you've already touched on this, there is the much less talked about issue of declining sexual potency. Sex therapists say 70 per cent of men in their seventies, 80 per cent in their eighties and

90 per cent in their nineties have lost their sexual potency. If men have equated masculinity or even their sense of self with sexual potency, then its decline is a huge shock, a huge disappointment and a major source of grumpiness that can scarcely be mentioned – especially not to other blokes.

'There are other factors too, but they apply equally to women and men. They're the broader health issues associated with ageing – loss of independence, the death of a spouse and friends and perhaps an associated fear of death itself. And, of course, the very real sense that as we get older, we are running out of time to do the things we want to do. There are no new beginnings, so it doesn't leave us with much to look forward to.'

~

No new beginnings to look forward to.

I wonder how many of you feel that sentence encapsulates exactly what makes you feel grumpy?

And who could blame you?

But perhaps we can do something about that.

~

Now comes the Dorothy Dixer from me. I stand up like the Honourable Member for Blokes Everywhere and ask the Prime Minister of Being a Good Bloke this: so, Hugh, how should we best respond to the onset of grumpiness?

He is clearly delighted and very well prepared.

'Geoff, grumpiness is a form of self-absorption. Yet deep life-satisfaction – the good life, the life of goodness – is all about service to others, sensitivity to others' needs, concern for others' wellbeing. It's our willingness to make sacrifices for the common good that marks us out as truly human. It is our capacity for creating and maintaining social harmony that explains why we alone – among the five species of human that once roamed the planet – survived and prospered.'

In just a moment, Hugh will utter a phrase that, frankly, makes my heart sing. Go on, Hugh ...

'Some archaeologists explain it as "survival of the kindest".'

Survival of the ...?

'Kindest.'

Hugh explains further: 'All of which encourages us to take the focus off "me", yet we live in a Me culture at present. When older people complain about the self-centredness of the young, they should first look in the mirror. If you're a grump, you're probably as guilty of self-centredness as any young person trying to find their way.'

So, Hugh, are you asking us blokes to explore our vulnerability? Our ... feelings?

'Geoff, that is the key to it all! It is our emotional vulnerability that equips us for the virtues that help us establish harmonious communities and societies. Kindness, compassion, mutual respect, a willingness to listen even to those with whom we disagree. As Samuel Johnson wrote: "Kindness is in our power even when fondness is not."

'We need to recognise that vulnerability makes us strong, not weak. We're mortal, after all, and our legacy will not be about what job we did or how many arguments we won, but about how kind and considerate we were or weren't. How loving to our family, how kind to our neighbours, how loyal to our friends, how committed to building social cohesion.'

I must pause.

What he is asking of us is not arduous, nor should it make us feel self-conscious or unsure. He is merely inviting us to engage and bask in the glow that can come with it.

Hugh, I know you have spent your working life talking to people about who they are and how they see the world, so I have to ask, how do you see it today, as an older man?

'I've been very fortunate, as a social researcher, to be on the frontiers of social change. I couldn't ignore what was happening, especially on the gender front, but also with the IT revolution and the economic revolution, and if I showed any signs of not keeping up, my sons would soon give me a gentle nudge in the right direction.

'Apart from all that, the death of many of my closest friends, four in the past year, has taught me a great deal about the fragility and impermanence of life, and the need for more attentive and empathic listening as the key to rich, enduring personal relationships.

'So I think, I hope, I've gradually changed in the direction of being a genuine "gender egalitarian" and a person who values everyone for their humanity.'

And we do that by ...?

Hugh says the secret lies in embracing just one word. He repeats it three times for effect.

'Connections! Connections! Connections!

'I'm enjoying deeper life satisfaction than ever due to the richness of my personal relationships. After all, grumpiness is usually a sign that we're taking ourselves too seriously, and that's a very isolating frame of mind.

'In practical terms, it's my personal connections that keep me growing and changing. My wife, my family, my friends – especially some newer, younger friends who have emerged in the wake of the loss of so many contemporaries. Spending time with younger people – whether friends, neighbours, children and grandchildren – is a great way to postpone fossilisation!'

~

I have had so many conversations with Hugh Mackay over the years, and each time they end, I feel as if he is offering me the wisest words and the warmest grandfatherly hug. He sees hope and possibility in every day. He is curious and caring. And he believes in 'survival of the kindest'.

Chapter 19

Regrets

'Regrets, I've had a few, but then again, too few to mention ...'

Was Frank Sinatra a smug bastard or did he just know how to move on?

~

One of the challenges of producing this little handbook of helpful tips for blokes who don't even know they want them is to explore what's most likely to resonate. What approaches might help you, me or us fight off the inclination to focus on the negative?

I've talked about the need to see the GP regularly, and even about the impact of declining testosterone, if only to reassure you that what's happening to you is happening to me and every other bloke as well. A slight diminution over time of our superpowers.

Our mental health is important too. Knowing what the warning signs are when we begin to feel a little shaky. It's also an area of specialised medicine and I'd best defer to those with the keenest insights.

In the meantime, you may find value in taking yourself off to the

Beyond Blue website (https://www.beyondblue.org.au) for a look around and possibly to answer an online questionnaire about why you might be feeling flat.

We are getting better at talking about it. And should you bring it up with your GP today, you may well be the third or fourth patient to do so.

~

This book is just me trying to prod a bit, provoke a bit and encourage you *a lot* to find more positive pathways. And there is one major contributing factor to our health and happiness that I do want to talk about.

Regret.

And how we live with it. How, after a lifetime, we understand and evaluate it. And how we might learn to reconcile and accept it.

Have you had a few? Regrets?

What's this 'too few to mention' bullshit, Frank? Surely, over life we accumulate hundreds of them, big and small, profound and idiotic. And they weigh on us. The distress and sorrow over decisions we made or didn't make. The things we said or didn't say. The fork in the road that sent us in the wrong direction.

Regrets. We all have them. Probably too many to mention, Frank.

How we choose to deal with those memories is going to have a significant impact on our state of mind today, tomorrow and probably twenty years from now. Do we reflect on lessons learnt and find some comfort or reassurance? Or do we still pick over those fateful moments again and again?

About the time we made the wrong call. Said yes when we should have said no. Stood back when our help was needed. Walked away when things got hard. Came on too strong. Chose the wrong option. Made things worse. Didn't care enough. Allowed someone to be hurt.

Flip some of those sentences around. Perhaps we should have stood back or said yes or been more assertive, not less. Different versions of the same. In all, an explosion of judgements, choices, snap decisions, brain fades and impetuous moments, both wilful and accidental, that we humans impose on one another – across every second of every day of our lives. The moments we stuff up, mess up, get wrong, misjudge.

I bet you can list them too.

We all can. Often in order of disastrous consequence.

~

Peter McEvoy is a professor of clinical psychology at Curtin University. Years ago, I used to talk to him a lot on the wireless. He's got a pretty good grasp of what's going on inside our heads and seems remarkably composed and even reassuring about what he sees in there.

'Geoff, we all live with regrets. It is human, unless you're a certified psychopath. It means you have values, that you care about your values and about other people, and you are a person with some compassion. These are all admirable qualities. And regret is an emotion that provides information. And it may be useful information, if the regret is truly ours to bear.'

By way of example, Professor McEvoy explains that he might ask a client to create a list of factors that contributed to an outcome of regret. 'We list all of them. Then, within a pie chart, we start attributing proportions of "blame" for the outcome to each of them, saving the client's portion until last. We are interested in knowing what portion is left over for them at the end. It can sometimes help put things into perspective and to be sure that the level of regret and guilt is proportionate.'

That's worth remembering as we reflect on our failings, isn't it?

Is our level of regret and guilt proportionate? It often isn't. We tend to wind it up to eleven when a six out of ten might be a more accurate account of the impact of our actions.

From what I've read, part of the psychology behind regret relies on something called counterfactual thinking. A focus, often unrealistic, on what might have been, had we not stuffed up, rather than what actually happened in the aftermath of that stuff-up. So the cause of much regret is the belief, often without any evidence to support it, that life would have been so much better had we made the other decision. We do it all the time.

Might my chance meeting with Paul McCartney back in 1989 have blossomed into a duet and Christmas number-one song, if only I'd held his attention for a bit longer and been a bit more interesting (and could sing)? If only I hadn't failed the Groundlings improv-comedy course in Los Angeles a few years later, might I have hosted the Oscars this year? Might the *Titanic* not have sunk, if only the crew had access to a pair of binoculars?

What?

Not a bad example really. What do you think was the reason for the sinking of the *Titanic*? Of course. It struck an iceberg that no one saw it until it was too late. Apparently, before the *Titanic* set sail, its second officer, David Blair, left the ship and took with him a key to the locker that contained his binoculars. Consequently, the *Titanic*'s lookout did not have access to a pair of binoculars.

People have speculated. 'If only' those binoculars had been made available, the iceberg may have been seen earlier, and 1500 people need not have died, and a film with Leonardo DiCaprio and Kate Winslet need not have been made. But the 'If only ...' question can't be proven. It can only be speculated upon.

And what about all the other considerations? The ship hit the iceberg at night – how useful would binoculars have been in the dark? And what about the brittle fractures in the hull's steel? Or the rivets that failed and popped? Or the not-so-tight watertight compartments that enabled the ship to flood quickly? Or the fact some passengers left their bloody portholes open?

And so the unsinkable sank.

I wonder if David Blair had regrets about forgetting to hand over the key to the locker that would have made his binoculars available. Or would he have had regrets about media headlines many years after his death that asked, 'Is this the man who sank the *Titanic*?'

I hope you can rest easier, David. I reckon the answer is no, you did not sink the *Titanic*.

~

Lots of us come to be defined by our regret and the 'If only ...' questions that we ponder. But let's be realistic. How many of these questions can be tested and answered? Is the endless reappraisal doing anything other than keeping us awake at night?

If only I hadn't prioritised work so much. If only I'd spent more time with the kids when they were growing up. If only Dad had found a way to tell me he loved me. If only I could have told my boys the same thing.

If only I hadn't tried so hard to fulfil everyone's expectations. If only I'd given them the bloody key so they could have grabbed the binoculars.

Professor McEvoy describes the futility of counterfactual thinking.

'The what ifs? If only? They are completely unhelpful.

'There is a psychology professor in the UK called Ed Watkins who has done a lot of work on the type of rumination that leads people into a dark place of depression. It turns out that counterfactual – what he calls abstract – thinking, such as what ifs, only increases the risk of depression. What he calls more concrete thinking – "What can I do about it?" or "How can I fix this right now?" – is much less likely to cause unnecessary distress, and it is more productive.'

To have less distress and to be more productive. Look at the appeal and power of those words. The opportunity to learn rather than to keep punishing ourselves.

We also need to remember, I think, that when we choose to continue to punish ourselves – because we have determined that we deserve it – there will often be collateral damage. To those we love. To those who love us. Our personally destructive behaviour will hurt others.

~

Of course, some of our actions do have profound and life-altering consequences. I, probably like you, have experienced and continue to live with a serious regret. I didn't do anything wrong. And I can rationalise it. I can excuse myself. I simply didn't see something as it unfolded. And yet I don't think it will ever quite let go of its hold over me.

But maybe that's for me to live with.

It was a wintry Sunday night in April 2006 in our suburban home in Melbourne's east. Nearly dinner time. I was in the kitchen, kneeling and peering into the oven to check on a chicken tomato bake I was cooking.

What I didn't know was that on the other side of the benchtop, my eight-year-old son, Hugh, was trying to open a bag of apples. With a pair of scissors.

And while my back was turned, in an action of absurd precision, he managed not to cut open the plastic bag, but to stab himself in the right eye with one of the scissor prongs.

It destroyed his cornea.

Had I not had my back to him, Hugh would not have lost the sight in his right eye. Had I not had my back to him, Hugh would not have had to endure an incredible trauma. If only I had turned around. If only he'd asked me to get him an apple.

Nineteen years on. If only …?

How'd you like that regret, Franky? Worthy of a mention? You smug, Mafia-loving, Nixon-supporting, women-hating motherfucker.

Eighteen years on, I can tell you that Hugh is – as you will soon, I hope, ascertain from his own writing – a smart, funny, well-adjusted adult who obviously has to look very carefully when he changes lanes while driving. It's not for me to assume that an 'If only …' assessment of Hugh's accident would have changed his life for the better. He's gone okay. Better than okay. He has endured and he has built resilience.

He is the apple of my …

Don't say it.

~

Regrets

On a good day, on most days, I know that is enough. And on other days, I feel sad and acknowledge a great regret. And a personal failing.

But something positive happened too. These days, for whatever reason, I feel I possess an intense and intuitive radar that scans Hugh, wherever he is in the world, for signs of his health and happiness. A deep, resonant awareness. And it's reassuring.

To which he might reply, and with wry comic effect, 'Little bit late for that, Dad, don't you think?'

And we both know the answer is yes.

Regrets. The biggest of my life. But manageable. Most days.

~

What about you? How are you able to process a lifetime of decisions and judgements and calls, good and bad?

We can pause if you like.

~

We should also recognise – and not beat ourselves about the head with sticks over the fact – that sometimes we just do dumb things. Things we might recall today with a 'What was I thinking?' shake of the head.

Like the day, about fifty years ago, I inexplicably punched my Grade Six friend Kim in the stomach during afternoon playtime at Kalamunda Primary School. It was such a lousy thing to do. I remember Kim's tall frame went down like a collapsing building, and while I don't think I hit him with a particularly brutal right, I can't for the life of me understand why I did it in the first place.

Frankly, I can't for the life of me understand why I'm still trying to validate the experience by saying I didn't hit him that hard!

And because it was such a mean thing to do, and because I have other memories of liking this gentle-natured kid, the image of his face sagging in such shock and dismay has stayed with me forever. And so it should.

Professor McEvoy explains why. 'That image of Kim's face, and the emotional reaction you felt at that time, have become fused. When the image intrudes into your consciousness, the emotion linked to that image is reactivated – neurons that fire together, wire together. If you had not seen Kim's face at that moment, and rather just thought about having hit him, it would be unlikely to pack the same emotional punch.'

Which it still does. So that's not going to leave me anytime soon, then, is it? Fair enough.

Over the years, I've even put out calls to Kim on ABC Radio while discussing the subject of regret, in the hope of offering a public apology. There has been no response. And until he hears it from me, I am not forgiven or exonerated and may never be. And maybe I am not right to presume his forgiveness anyway? And so the memory of my action follows me. A faint but ever-present shadow of an unkind act that I am still hoping to apologise for.

A regret. Albeit a regret Frank probably wouldn't bother to mention.

~

Professor McEvoy has been listening patiently. He knows people generally want to make good.

'If someone is sure the regret is theirs to carry, they could consider how to try and fix it. Not just for the other person, but for themselves. We repair relationships by accepting responsibility – where responsibility is yours – and providing reparation when it is required. We do what needs to be done. But it is not always possible to repair what was done in the past.

'Geoff, your personal anecdotes are good examples. The only option we have is to change the way we think about the situation and ourselves. Might it be possible to interpret that pang of regret as sign of personal development and a reminder of all that we have learnt?

'And it also acknowledges what it means to be human. Imperfect. Learning. Growing. That's the best we can really hope for.'

Still, Kim, if you're out there ...

I am really, really sorry.

~

Is it just a human thing, I wonder? To pick the sore of a mistake and rub it raw because of some weird determination that suffering is all we deserve?

I've been considering the male panda by way of example. Well, I just saw another one on the news. Will it spend long hours – now the end is near and he faces the final curtain – sitting among the bamboo and ruminating on the mistakes he has made? Does he feel regret that after getting some female panda he barely knew pregnant, he abandoned her to raise the cub alone? Does he ever wonder how the kid got on? Does he ever look at himself in a mirror and acknowledge that yes, he is very fat and unmotivated? Does he stare at his disproportionately small penis and feel inadequate? Does he wince? Does his conscience prick? Does he feel the ache of regret?

In case you are wondering, the answer is probably no. The panda is at his happiest doing fuck-all and thinking about nothing other than his next meal. And while he has a life that for some of us, frankly, has a certain appeal, we humans are somehow a lot more accountable for the decisions we make in our lives.

So for those of you who right now might be dealing with the argument that sent your daughter out of the slammed front door ... Or have just traipsed mud through the front of the house because you forgot to wipe your feet on the mat ...

Let regret come with apology and understanding.

If we can't be allowed to learn from our mistakes, even in our latter years, then regret serves no useful purpose. It only returns us to the scene of our failures and plays them on a loop. There is no compassion in that endless retelling and no opportunity for wider context or apology. It becomes all about us.

Best advice? Stay away from posing too many questions to which there is no answer. Do not indulge a gloomy day by seeking to rub your personal history raw; it won't change anything. Be curious about an 'If only ...' question, but know its limitations. Understand life's regrets without becoming a slave to them.

And buy your apples in paper bags.

Oh, I did ask Professor McEvoy if he thinks pandas have regrets.

'Geoff, I have no idea if pandas feel regret. Out of my area of expertise, I'm afraid. My hunch is that regret is peculiar to our overactive prefrontal cortex.'

~

There is a fella I once met who it seems to me paid a terrible price for his feelings of regret. And they must have dogged him for more than sixty years. His name was Dunc Gray. Dunc won Australia's only gold medal in cycling at the 1932 Los Angeles Olympics.

I did a feature story on him, when he was in his early nineties. Dunc was incredibly proud of his bike-riding career, but one thing gnawed at him terribly. He was also the flag-bearer for Australia at the Berlin Olympic Games of 1936.

'I was this far away from him,' he told me, stretching out his arms. 'I coulda skewered him with me flag. I was this close.'

The him he wanted to skewer was Adolf Hitler.

And even if modern measuring technology might suggest Dunc probably wasn't quite close enough to affect his intended javelin throw or fencing thrust, his sense of despair remained.

Imagine spending more than half a century believing you might have averted a world war.

'I coulda skewered him.'

Some regrets have to be let go.

Chapter 20

Giving the Future a Try

Now I should warn you, Chapter 21 contains terrifying revelations. In it, I discuss the hitherto never dared spoken of, minding-bending reality that we are all going to die. All of us.

The idea might be alarming to you, but please don't jump ahead in a state of panic, or out a window. We're not there yet, and you're looking really well. For a bloke your age.

This is Chapter 20, and all kinds of interesting things might happen. In our short-to-medium-term future.

~

I'm interested to know how you perceive the enormity of that concept, 'the future'.

What does it look like for you? Thrilling? Tedious? Short?

And I guess we all want to know, but sometimes don't dare ask – what role will we be given to play?

When we are kids, the future is boundless, timeless, beyond imagination and filled only with endless possibility and wonder. We believe we can do and be anything. Superheroes and popstars and nurses. Rulers of mighty empires or owners of our own petting zoo. We can cure the sick with hospitals made from Lego and medicine made from jelly beans, slide down rainbows, ride on a lion's back through the jungle or stab monsters through the brain with our mighty swords. We can do anything.

Until, of course, the future arrives and chooses someone else for all the really good gigs. We, with very few exceptions, do not become popstars or superheroes. We become account managers and roof tilers.

When I was a kid in the 1960s, the future belonged to cartoon depictions of George and Jane Jetson, curiously living a suburban American life but in space. Soon enough, I thought, that's where we would all be, dashing about the heavens in flying cars.

Hasn't happened.

In the early 1970s, I remember a *Reader's Digest* article told me of a highly industrialised and mechanised future in which all the hard graft would be done by robots, leaving us free to pursue lives of idle leisure. My daughter and her husband do have one of those self-propelled, vaguely sentient vacuum cleaners that bump into furniture and scare the shit out of the dog, but are they now lying on a banana lounge in the pool drinking cocktails? No, they're not. Not yet. Maybe they never will.

When I entered my twenties in the 1980s and became increasingly interested in Australia's place in the world, I assumed that one day, not too far away, we would shrug off our colonial yoke and proudly become a republic. I'm still waiting for us to stop tugging the forelock and believing Prince Andrew ever went to a Pizza Express in Woking.

And on April 1st of 1995 – yes, April Fool's Day – I took my wife and my not-yet-two-year-old daughter to the MCG to watch the Fremantle Dockers play their first game of AFL football, against Richmond. We lost by just five points, and I wondered with delicious anticipation how many premierships we would win over the coming decades. I am still waiting for the first one.

And as I age, it has now dawned on me that it is entirely possible I will never see a Dockers premiership. Or an Australian republic. Or technology truly freeing people from the enslavement of chores. Or a flying car.

And given life's 'premiership window' is indeed closing a little each year, no wonder we become vulnerable to an attack of the grumps. Many of the dreams we had were not realised. Expectations were not met. And the stupidity and failings of the world were not corrected. Only repeated.

Frankly, there is daily evidence to suggest the future doesn't look very promising. In recent days, I have read about high-school girls from Bacchus Marsh Grammar in Victoria being targeted by deepfake porn. I barely even understand that sentence.

Apparently, their images were grotesquely sexualised by the manipulation of AI technology and sent into the lascivious lives of strangers online, humiliating the teenage girls. It's part of that misogynistic ideology I referred to earlier, espoused by the Andrew Tate figures of this world, encouraging young men to dismiss, ridicule and reduce women to subservience. New technology being weaponised against women. Your partner, your daughter or granddaughter or Tamsin, that nice little kid next door.

Is this really what the future looks like?

Giving the Future a Try

I've also been reading how AI is providing Chinese women with relationship options beyond marrying flabby Mùchén or chain-smoking Hàoyú. His name is Dan, and he is not real. He is a ChatGPT invention who is apparently kind and empathetic and a good listener – and, frankly, what girl wouldn't go for that after a hard day at work?

Now, we blokes might take some solace from the fact Dan is definitely a dud root, because he does not exist as a physical manifestation. But he will eventually. And he probably won't be a dud root.

Do you remember MrBeast in Chapter 5? The YouTube sensation who began his career counting from one to 100,000 on camera? He recently came to Sydney, where he organised a viral stunt outside the Opera House. Thousands of people turned up to watch him give away ten cars, among them a Lamborghini. Do you remember how many YouTube followers he had in Chapter 5? It was 233 million then. It's 290 million now.

That is what fame looks like today, and this is what you do to be famous.

And to end this bulletin of thoroughly modern news ...

Taylor Swift has just closed a concert at Wembley Stadium by exhorting her fans to scream, by way of farewell, 'Fuck the patriarchy!' Not just a political statement, but a lyric from one of her best-known songs.

~

Having trouble processing all this? Wondering if these situations, scenarios and characters are to become the faces and voices that shape the attitudes of the future?

History tells us that some will. Others will drift and fade. Some will fill us with hope. Some with despair.

And whatever happens, we have to get used to the idea that we no longer get to decide it.

And yet it seems that just a few years ago we were the ones shouting instructions, thumping the table, pulling the levers and wearing the accidental birthright privilege of being us.

But things change. Others are running the show.

And the irrefutable truth about the future? It will arrive whether we engage with it or not.

How do you consider What Comes Next? Do you marvel at it? Do you fear it? Are you dumbfounded by the pace of it?

I imagine the answer is yes on many counts.

And while our own ability to change the course of mighty rivers or bend steel with our bare hands or run faster than a speeding bullet has been somewhat compromised by a dodgy hip, I reckon we blokes still have a role to play. And it is not just that of curmudgeon.

I'm not suggesting we can stop the manipulation of artificial intelligence by bad actors, or prevent a future where our granddaughter, in lieu of finding a partner in real life, chooses a caring chatbot instead – but we can stay connected. We can still give a damn, even when all our instincts just want to shout, 'The world has gone bloody mad!'

We have choices. Some of us might believe we have nothing more to offer and will retreat further into the shadows, the comfort of our memories, how it used to be. But that is a small space. And it doesn't invite many visitors. I think you've probably gathered by now that I think nostalgic yearnings can rather blanket the prospects of a bright new day.

Or we can instead take out a folding chair, plonk it right in the middle of all the unfolding chaos and declare that whatever happens next, we want to be here to see it. Maybe not quite the active participant we once were, but a very engaged eyewitness still.

~

How do we do it?

I want to seek the opinion of someone with real insight. I'm not talking so much about Mystic Meg or Alexander the Crystal Seer or readers of tea leaves; I'm talking about futurists. Those who study the data, the science and the trends to forecast where we are headed and what it might be like when we get there.

Michael McQueen is a social researcher, a change strategist, an author and a globally much-in-demand public speaker. I want to ask him how we blokes might best prepare for and make sense of the incredible technological change that is swirling around us. And how we, as we get older, can stay informed and involved and enthused by all that possibility.

Michael, unsurprisingly, loves the subject and is generous with his time.

'Geoff, men are used to being useful. And valuable. And knowing how things work. They can fix things. They know how organisations and businesses run. The challenge for them is that increasingly this is a world in which they don't know how it works. The truth is, most young people don't know either. They just have the confidence to go with the uncertainty.'

Michael gives the example of ChatGPT – a language-processing bit of AI that has been around for a few years now. Seemingly an extraordinary tool for educators and businesses, it essentially harvests words by scanning the internet for information you ask for and returns it to you in sentences you might have written yourself. It promises inspiration and greater productivity and can write emails and compose poems.

Such technologies are revolutionising the way we work, learn and play. Apparently.

Curiously, this very morning I downloaded ChatGPT to my phone and became immediately overwhelmed when I read that it 'Promises to answer all questions'. It even offered to 'create inspiring quotes with visual themes'. I considered asking it to produce 'Fuck off, you monster!' with the visual theme of a kid stabbing it in the brain with a mighty sword, but chose not to engage.

Desperate not to leave any of my DNA or the stench of my fear, I then uninstalled it before it could sink its laser-like claws into my very being. Because it scares me.

I think this is the point Michael is making.

'It is! Most people have no clue how ChatGPT works. They use it, but they have no clue how it works. Older generations, because they are unfamiliar, are less likely to tinker with things and learn how to use those tools, whereas younger generations are more likely to have a go. They don't understand how it works; they just know how to make it work for them. It's the willingness to give things a try that is the key here.'

Michael also wants to remind us that this caution or unwillingness to engage with the new is a pretty familiar response to it.

'There was the generation that said, "I'll never use an ATM because I can't trust them. I want to go into a branch with a bankbook." Each generation tends to scoff at the previous one. So there's nothing new; it's just the pace of change today that is so great.

'The sad thing from my perspective is that a lot of the older generation are just checking out too early. They're saying, "I'm just going to retreat to my little clique and gather together and complain about how the world is going to pot."

'I don't see it that way. I think there is an opportunity to stay engaged, ask questions and be available to offer wisdom. They may not be able to offer tech advice, but I tell you what, they've come through a few financial downturns, they know how to weather a divorce when running a small business and how to recalibrate your life when you get a cancer diagnosis in your forties. They know those things.

'They have seen some life and the wisdom that comes from it. It is hard to overstate how valuable that is, but sadly a lot of the older generation are assuming, "Well, I can't do the technology, I've got nothing to offer," which is just not true.'

Michael believes dramatic change is scaring us more than it should. Take ChatGPT again – for some of us it elicits fascination and for others fear. Michael clearly loves it.

'These tools can do things as if by magic. The ability to go to ChatGPT and say, "I'm driving from Perth to Broome. I've got seven or eight days. What is the best itinerary? What should I see along the way?" And within twenty-three seconds, it will give you better advice than a travel agent who has been in the industry for thirty-five years. The level of knowledge and acuity is incredible.

'If I was to sum it up,' says Michael, 'the challenge for anyone, really, is how to keep the balance of certainty and curiosity. And I completely get it that in a world which is changing fast, there is a natural desire to cling to what we know and cling to what is certain. But it will mean we will miss out on a lot of things that will make our lives objectively a whole lot easier if you are willing to be curious and try things that are new and unfamiliar.

'The beauty of curiosity is that you are more interested in asking questions than giving answers. I think about this all the time. How much of my time is spent formulating opinions on things, judgements on things, rather than trying to understand them? Curiosity rather than certainty is the best guiding principle, rather than retreating when the world seems scary.'

I really like this guy. For him, technology is still our servant rather than our overlord. He is naturally very curious and broadly optimistic. But Michael also concedes that not all change is good.

There is, he says, a reason why we put seatbelts in cars and warning labels on cigarettes and banned the use of asbestos. Wisdom, he says, dictates that when something is just not good for us, we need to moderate, alter or stop our use of it. And he adds that social-media and phone use among young people may well be the most pressing example of where that need sits today.

Indeed, not long after our conversation, the federal government announced its intention to legislate a ban on social media for younger Australians. The great debate will be about how old a kid should be before being free to engage with it, but the intent is clear. Not all technology and not all change is in the public good. Sometimes we have to call a halt.

~

I feel better for talking to Michael, but, just between you and me, I am a bit dubious of the claim that a newly invented piece of technology is better equipped to plan a Perth-to-Broome holiday than an experienced travel agent.

Long after our discussion, I download ChatGPT again and ask it that very question. Within twenty-three seconds, I have a suggested itinerary in front of me. It is comprehensive and, to quote the text, 'provides a mix of coastal views, national parks, wildlife encounters and memorable experiences along the way'.

I've decided not to uninstall the app.

What will the future be like? Well, I've got out the folding chair and intend to plonk myself down in the middle of it. And the words of Michael McQueen are ringing in my ears.

'The willingness to give things a try.'

Repeat that. Make it a mantra.

Or if you're feeling adventurous, make it an inspirational ChatGPT quote with a picture of you – trying.

Chapter 21

Death

One hundred years from now, we will all be dead. And so will our children. And our dog. Even Rupert Murdoch will be dead (probably). Everyone we ever met, liked or loathed will be gone. Almost everyone born on Planet Earth this very morning will have died too.

Any memories and fond recollections of us will, in all likelihood, no longer exist. Oh sure, there might be the odd smudgy digital fingerprint pulled down from the long-abandoned 'cloud' by a forensic historian. And maybe they will find that hilarious Facebook video of you vomiting in a bin at the 2008 Melbourne Cup. You might then appear as a flash frame of olden-day human vulgarity in a clip show, to roars of laughter from an audience of holograms or robot dogs. But will anyone remember it is you?

Just between us, I do remain slightly hopeful that my three-second appearance in a crowd scene in the Robert Altman film classic of 1992, *The Player*, will survive in a library of motion-picture history somewhere. But even then, I doubt anyone will go in search of it. And the role is uncredited. No one will know it is me.

As John Cleese once put it, in comedic Shakespearian tones about a dead parrot, we will truly Cease To Be.

There is something tumultuous about the observation, though, isn't there? The mathematical certainty that there will be no trace of us left. That this life we live so furiously, or which we, even now, continue to fret about, will largely be forgotten.

And when that rather miserable truth is pointed out to us, we know it to be true, but we generally don't like to think about it. We'd prefer not to know.

Do you give much thought to what your final farewell will look like? When it's the end of your world as you know it?

For some of us, there is the promise of God's merciful judgement and eternal rest among fluffy pillows of cloud. Probably pomegranates as well. Lots of pomegranates. Some of us hope we will be reunited with those we have loved and lost, like Aunty Avis, who worked in the ladies' lingerie section at Coles New World in the 1970s and was a particular favourite of mine.

Some martyrs believe, I think mistakenly, that seventy-two virgins await them. And, of course, if we have lived wicked lives, then there are various versions of Hell into which we will be cast. Some of us imagine we will return as something else. No one ever thinks it will be as mosquito larvae in brackish pond water. Usually an eagle soaring ever higher on the currents of a beautiful blue-sky day. Or a dolphin. Or Florence Nightingale.

And then there are others – well, people like me – who think nothing much happens at all, beyond a bizarre human biology experiment and whatever we can find in a dress-up box. It requires us – the dead – to be pumped full of embalming fluid and liberally sprinkled with baby powder so the pong isn't too fruity and we don't return to nature too quickly. After which, wads of cottonwool are placed in our mouths, not for the opportunity to do our incomparable Vito Corleone impression, but to fill our cheeks with that modest 'it's actually quite comfy here' smile. And we are dressed, ironically enough, as if we are about to go out to a dinner dance. In a dark suit or a lovely frock and with our hair combed and styled just so.

We are dead, but this is a public depiction to confirm to others that we seem okay about it. We don't appear terrified. Those who have loved us get to peer in and say how peaceful we look, even though, to be fair, the morticians have gone a bit heavy on the rouge.

And as our lives are remembered, they will laugh and weep and then sing along to 'Always Look on the Bright Side of Life' or something similar, as we prepare to be buried in a box or burnt in an absolute roaster of an oven, while they take tea and sandwiches. Egg sandwiches.

~

The great unknowable. What will the end be like?

It seems to send a chill through many of us, doesn't it?

Well, how about returning to those provocative truths at the start of this chapter? The mathematical certainty of our demise within a very particular period of time. To me, it's just that. Maths. And what it provides is clarity and context and opportunity.

It reminds me how small and fleeting my life is and absolutely confirms that I really don't have a lot of time here and, consequently, why would I – or anyone else – want to use that time being an arsehole?

What the maths does is bring into clear view the count-it-down reality that we have lived *this* long ... and perhaps have ... *that* long to go.

I'm guessing and hoping I may be lucky enough to have maybe another twenty-five years of this rewarding and broadly satisfying life. Or I might have an aneurysm over breakfast tomorrow and drown in a puddle of crunchy nut clusters.

I don't know. We don't know. But it does make the compelling case to live our best lives.

And the best life, even with the bar of expectation set low, might simply be defined as one in which we can find some measure of satisfaction that we've done okay. No self-sabotage. No 'If only ...' regret. The comfort of having given life a good shot. And been kind to others along the way.

Because ... as if this point has not already been made a thousand times ... being a grumpy bugger takes energy. And if we only have another twenty-five years left or we're facing the immediate reality of a crunchy nut catastrophe, where's the value in expending all that effort on perpetuating life's negatives?

Using valuable time finding fault in others. Using valuable time probing weakness in the belief it validates our own strength. Using valuable time needing to be right all the time.

What's the point? The numbers are in. Life's too short.

~

I was delighted to read today of a new survey about those of us who scream and shout and beat our chests like wounded apes, and its conclusion that none of that behaviour seems to help reduce our unhappiness. We already know that shouting at the umpire, screaming at the bloke in the Camry or threatening to do something unimaginably unkind to Mrs Drobny's Lhasa Apso might make us feel satisfied and righteous for a moment, but an Ohio State University examination of more than 150 studies and more than 10,000 participants couldn't find any evidence that it does anything other than make us ...

Angrier.

And grumpier.

~

So why not go and do some slow flow yoga? Or meditate. Or do some diaphragmic breathing. Or go and buy yourself a family pack of Smarties and eat all of them.

The last piece of advice is mine. I don't know what slow flow yoga is, but will presume it is completely unnecessary for men of dignity.

Just understand that the science is in and the maths has been done. And we've only got a while left. It might be quite a while or it might be tomorrow morning over breakfast.

~

Today I'm meeting a friend and an outstanding human. His name is Professor Bruce Robinson.

Bruce is a big shambling bear of a man with a brilliant, restless mind and the kindest of hearts. A respiratory-medicine specialist and cancer researcher, he, along with his teams, has helped reshape how we understand and treat lung cancer and asbestos-related disease. And it was after talking to dying patients – indeed, he has often had to deliver the saddest of news to them – that Bruce began the Fathering Project, which has now established many hundreds of dads' groups in Australian schools, there to provide a framework of support and engagement, to remind men that there's so much more to life than their traditional role as breadwinner. (As mentioned in Chapter 1, I've been an ambassador for the Fathering Project for the last few years. It's brilliant.)

I have come to see Bruce to learn something more of those conversations about death and dying and what happens to a man when he is told he has a shadow on his lung and only a short time to live. Bruce is at home, wearing jeans and an old windcheater, looking as if he's just woken from a winter's hibernation. The hug is bearlike too.

He is a man of faith, and when I open with my chirpy observation that a hundred years from now we'll all be dead, he comes back with a biblical verse.

'Teach us to number our days that we may get a heart of wisdom.'

That was Moses, apparently, from about 3500 years ago, telling us we're not going to live forever, so we better hope we've learnt some of the important stuff along the way. And not waste time doing things that don't matter.

'And that's my feeling at the moment,' says the seventy-four-year-old scientist, reclining now on a well-worn sofa. 'I'm getting older and you never know when the sword is going to fall. So what do you want to get done, and has anything been left unsaid?'

Bruce, tell me about these men you treat. And the very challenging and, I'm sure, sad conversations you have.

He manoeuvres a cushion to make himself more comfortable.

'Mate, I'm a lung specialist, and the most common lethal cancer is lung cancer, so I've had to break the bad news to hundreds and hundreds of people. This isn't palliative care at the back end, nor is it oncology in the middle. It's right at the front. The most poignant moment is when they sit there with their partner, hold hands, get the bad news and cry. They have just been told they're going to die.'

I ask Bruce how those men process that life-ending prognosis. He says it's important to tell them they have cancer. And that it has spread.

'That's the first thing I say. You do not say it's a tumour or something else, because they often don't understand. They'll smile and say, "Thank God it isn't cancer." So you have to be direct. And it's a sledgehammer word and it's going to send them into a whirl.' Bruce pauses. 'And sometimes I get teary as well, especially if they're young and they're not going to see their kids grow up. And then I wait a bit, usually reach my hand out and put it on their forearm or their shoulder.'

For a few patients there is denial, but Bruce says most accept the scientific reality, because diagnostic technologies are so precise these days.

It's an intrusive question, but I have to ask it. How soon do they ask Bruce, 'How long do I have left?' Do they want to know that straightaway?

'Mostly they do want to know. And I tell them exactly what the facts say. "Look, it could be as short as three months. The average is six months, but you could get maybe eighteen months, but there's a less than 10 per cent chance of that."'

Bruce uses a simple phrase to sum up their futures: 'Plan for the worst, but hope for the best.'

As he explains it, hoping for the best might mean eighteen months of life, much of it in reasonable health. Planning for the worst might be the reality that you have just twelve weeks to live. Hope for eighteen months, plan for twelve weeks.

I understand why Bruce likes to quote Moses. 'Teach us to number our days that we may get a heart of wisdom.' Time matters.

'This is where it gets visceral,' he explains. 'I tell them to get on and do things now. Do you want to go to Paris? Do it now. Don't wait until month number eleven or twelve, because you might not be well enough. Do it now.'

I ask Bruce, what do those men close to death speak about?

'It's always the same,' he says. 'Their regrets. That I didn't spend enough time with the kids.'

And Bruce has advice on that front too.

'I often ask them to think about writing some letters for their children or grandchildren to open on their sixteenth birthday or twenty-first birthday or whatever. To tell them the things you appreciate about them and your confidence in them and your aspirations for them. And I say, guaranteed, the tears will fall on the page and it's going to be very hard to do. You're going to look at a blank sheet, and say, "I don't want to do that."

'But let me tell you why it's good to do. Firstly: if you don't do it, you'll get too sick and you'll regret it and so will your partner. Those kids will get to sixteen or their twenty-first birthday and have nothing to read, nothing left of you.

'And number two: once you have done it, you're going to feel liberated. You've done it. And then every day from then on is a gift.'

Bruce pauses. He knows I'm a heathen, and something of a spiritual cynic, so he recounts the story of a friend of his who at the age of just fifty was struck down with lung cancer. This bloke was also a neighbour and now, in a wheelchair, was steered by his daughter around to Bruce's house for a catch-up.

Bruce asked him if there was anything he was afraid of. The friend said he was worried about a breathless and painful death. Bruce reassured him it wouldn't be like that.

The friend then asked a more poignant question: were his kids going to suffer emotionally because he died young?

'I said, mate, there'll forever be something missing in their lives. But in an ironic way, the way you have handled your dying, which is to spend time with them and talk to them and get them ready for it, is curiously going to enrich their lives. They'll become much more empathic, in a workplace or with friends, than they would have been otherwise. And of course they'd rather have you around, but it's not all bad. I think you can be reassured that they'll be better people, with more emotional intelligence through their lives, because of the way you've handled your death.'

Bruce believes it. He has witnessed it. Again and again.

There are good and bad ways to die.

'So,' he says, grinning now, 'in a hundred years' time, yes, mate, we will all be dead, but we might get to live on, because of the way in which we treat those people we love today.'

We hug again, and Bruce prepares to leave. He has a group of second-year medical students to lecture – about empathy.

And I am left, more than ever, believing that time and illness may lead to a diminution of who we think we are, and we may question our worth and value and relevance to others, but there is always wisdom and kindness to share. A legacy that will be remembered. And a life that wasn't forgotten.

When my Mum was in her last days, stricken by the respiratory consequences of many decades spent enjoying the extra-long smoothness of Rothmans Plain cigarettes, it was Bruce with his white coat and lumbering gait who walked into the dull-green twilight of her hospital ward, sat down by her bedside, whispered some quiet words and picked up her hand.

And held it tight.

Chapter 22

A Word from My Son

Now I've hopefully established my 'getting down with the kids' credentials – hanging out with the super-cool, super-thoughtful captain of the Fremantle Dockers and a remarkable young woman of extraordinary determination and courage – I appear to have no choice but to introduce you to another perspective on Australian men, as represented by my son, Hugh. Who is one. An Australian man, that is. A twenty-seven-year-old one.

Apparently, my editor is curious about a world view other than my own. And while I have strongly recommended that Hugh stop trying to ride on my literary coat-tails, he's been given a brief to consider what the world of his dad and *that* generation of the men looks like to him.

How similar is he to us, I wonder. How different? What does he like about us and what does he not? Will he feel some generational pressure to live as we have lived or will he eschew the uniforms and protocols of gendered expectation?

And, most importantly, will he put me in a tolerably nice nursing home? I can do no more now than walk away and leave you both to it.

A Word from My Son

~

Hello.

Dad has passed the reins over to me, his once prodigal son turned no-hoper, to tender some observations about issues affecting young men and what older Australians can learn from them. I'm not a sociologist, but neither is Geoff – although, as a journalist, he does think that's a comparable professional credential – which, of course, is the problem with journalism. So I'm here to offer my two cents.

If you'd like to read my full thoughts on the topic, my competing book, *A Bloke's Guide to Being a Completely Grumpy Young Bastard*, is now available in all good bookshops.

The generational divide between Australians is the subject of lamb ads, think pieces and housing crises. In many ways, it is a reflection of class imbalances as much as it is age – the perception that our democracy is a gerontocracy, with a pliable political class bending over backwards to serve up our country's immense wealth on a platter to geriatric landlords and ruddy-faced talkback radio audiences.

Do I think this is true? Yes!

My generation is on track to be the first generation to be substantially worse off than our parents, while standards of living will plummet further as deteriorating climate conditions threaten coastal areas, food security and general vibes. And none of us can find anywhere decent and affordable to call home.

It's conventional wisdom that people reject the politics of the generation that preceded them. Protesters marched against the Vietnam War in opposition to the conservative politics of their parents. They in turn became the arbiters of neoliberalism, and their own children duly took up the mantle of demonstrator against military interventions in Iraq and Afghanistan and, more recently, Gaza. This is, of course, a sweeping generalisation: like all conventional wisdom, it is mostly wrong.

My dad and I often have disagreements about politics. He rallies against a cynical world view that he feels is unproductive; I think that anyone who is against an immediate increase in JobSeeker should be forced to work split shifts in hospitality for the next ten years. But the values with which I was raised have stuck with me: equality, fairness and other lofty and commendable principles. Aren't I swell?

The differences in outlook are easy to explain. I am angry and discontented with our uncertain future; I fear for what the world will look like in twenty years. Dad knows what his future will look like – a retirement facility of my choosing.

There's an idea that 'kids today' – a phrase used as a pejorative by many older Australians and even some thirty-year-olds – are more sheltered than the generations that came before them. Sure, we may not muck about in pond scum for yucks or walk a half marathon without shoes to and from school every day, but did you? Did you really?

I'd argue the opposite is true – that kids today are more exposed to the world around them than ever before. The breakdown of traditional sources of community and belonging – accelerated in no small way by the pandemic – has forced young people to look outwards for social fulfilment.

The neighbourhood as a byword for the childhood experience is dead. Economic realities and structural inequality have made once-accessible hobbies and pastimes prohibitively expensive for struggling families. Community crime-watch groups on Facebook have made us more distrustful of our neighbours. Royal commissions have made us less likely to entrust our kids to strangers in strange institutions.

It's in the midst of this unfortunate reality that the internet has been the great disrupting force of the 21st century, a rich vein of opportunity to socialise, to belong and to play. The migration of community from physical to virtual spaces has brought with it endless possibilities, limited only by technology and imagination. No matter how niche an interest, there will be a dedicated forum of thousands who have committed untold hours to documenting and discussing it – they are the unknowing archivists of social movements, coin collecting and fetish pornography.

For young people, the internet offers a relatively anonymous space in which to explore interests and identity and to make friends. It's an outlet to talk about a show that none of your 'real' friends are watching. You might live across the world from the group of friends you play online games with, but it scratches the irresistible social itch, the same as hanging out at the movies. It might be a lifeline for someone struggling with their sexuality in a conservative or otherwise unwelcoming community.

This was the great promise of the internet as a democratising and equalising force. But no good thing can ever last. The vultures have descended, carving out its guts for profit, private interests and even more nefarious ends.

I've matured with the internet, which now provides me with an endless stream of content curated by algorithms designed to chew up as much of my time and attention as possible. I'm an adult. I can choose to apportion sixteen hours a day to reading and watching things that I know will reinforce my world view and make me cross – that's part of being a grown-up!

But what if I was ten years younger? What if my brain was still mouldable mush? Enter Andrew Tate; enter Jordan B. Peterson; enter the unending, unrelenting grift. Dad has already written about the rise of 'new' (read: stupid) conceptions of masculinity as espoused by people like Tate and Joe Rogan. If you've skipped the rest of the book and gone straight to my chapter (who could blame you?), I'll just say this: it's all about clout-chasing and money-making – but there are real-world consequences for their lack of principles. I am also, however, willing to entertain that Rogan might actually just be dumb as bricks, two wheels short of a bicycle etc.

In May 2024, as the nation was struggling with the epidemic of family and domestic violence that sees scores of women killed every year by husbands, fathers and other men known to them, Stephanie Wescott and Steven Roberts from Monash University wrote about how Andrew Tate's extremist views were becoming more prevalent, visible and dangerous in Australian schools. Their research found widespread abuse of female teachers and classmates across Australia, with primary- and high-school-age boys aping the misogyny and mannerisms of the manosphere influencer, alleged sex-trafficker and child sex offender.

I first heard of Tate a couple of years ago, shortly before his arrest in Romania. He was an internet celebrity who had gone completely unnoticed by me and my circle of terminally online friends: he had ten million followers on Twitter and by that point had over 11.6 billion views on TikTok, according to *The Guardian*. Why hadn't I heard of him? Because I was not fourteen. I was outside his target demographic.

So why are Australian young men and boys falling under the spell of extremists? Because Tate – and his myriad copycats, progenitors and pretenders – are offering a cure-all balm for society's ills, and they're not alone.

Boys coming of age in the 2020s have had their socialisation stunted by the pandemic and the erosion of in-person community. At this all-important stage of development, they're exposed to all sorts of shit that no reasonable parent would knowingly let their kids watch and be influenced by.

I'm not about to go all 'won't somebody please think of the children' here: I love the online content slop market, and I think platforms like TikTok can be really wonderful outlets for creativity and community, especially for young people. The (at time of writing) proposed ban on social media for kids is an insipidly blunt and misdirected bit of scared policymaking. It's the old adage of 'if all you have is a hammer, all your problems look like nails', except it ends with you hitting yourself in the nuts repeatedly.

But there's real evidence that kids are being groomed and radicalised by bad actors, aided by irresponsible tech companies and their inscrutable algorithms.

When I was a little kid, the hand-wringing over family values (or lack of) being represented on our television and cinema screens was a product of a much smaller media environment, with pop culture being dictated by a small group of media and production companies.

Parental guidelines and rating agencies exist to advise parents of what is and what is not appropriate for younger audiences. TV networks are also governed by broadcasting codes: think of the infamous 'turkey slap' episode of *Big Brother Australia* and how deeply it made John Howard furrow his formidable brows. In the internet age, however, with its focus on user-generated content, virality and loose restrictions on speech, it's much harder to moderate what content is available online and who can access it.

Age restrictions are laughably implemented. 'Yes, I am eighteen-plus and I would like to proceed to wonderfulasses.com.ru.'

Exhausted parents have naturally grown to rely on the endless trove of content available on the internet to keep their wee ones occupied for hours at a time, which has led some people to describe Generation Alpha (born 2011–2024) as 'iPad Kids'. I don't say this in judgement – Dad used to put a splash of gin in my orange juice to get me off to sleep – but when pre-teens have a more sophisticated understanding of how to use the internet than their parents, that makes monitoring their usage infinitely more difficult and risks exposing them to harmful content.

Not to mention that some of the content that is actually for kids on the internet is just fucking weird – there has been excellent reporting from *The New York Times* and others about how YouTube Kids has been hijacked by shady content producers that capitalise on the lucrative attention spans of babies and infants.

Andrew Tate's influence among Australian boys and young men is a perfect storm of terrible content moderation, big tech profiteering and brains that are still working out the finer points of critical thinking. Whether he genuinely believes the bile he spews, or if, as with the millions of other grifters, frauds and clout gainers, he is just another charlatan chasing a fortune, he is undoubtedly infecting young minds with an ideological sickness rooted in misogyny and conspiracy.

~

But they're not the only ones who are vulnerable: there's a warning here for older Australians too.

Australia has gone soft – too apologetic, too woke, too sensitive. Diversity has ravaged our institutions, from boardrooms to parliaments to movie screens. We used to be more fun, more carefree, more fair dinkum.

Except that's not actually true, is it?

I see the empty platitudes of an older generation as a rallying call to a meaner and less inclusive culture. I don't give a shit that we're not a bunch of larrikins anymore, or that meetings at work begin with an acknowledgement of country, or that I'm no longer guaranteed a cushy job because of my pasty skin and my outward-facing member. I do give a shit about my friends, and them being able to live comfortably in their own skin, identifying as they so choose. I give a shit about my girlfriend's mum having the opportunity to move from India as a nineteen-year-old and start a successful family-law practice. I give a shit about the future of this country – a future that should be compassionate and generous, as befitting our immense wealth and privilege.

But I understand that just as growing up can be an extremely isolating process, so too can growing older.

Much has been written about the 'male loneliness epidemic' and the difficulties men face in making new friends as they reach middle age and beyond. We are fragile in ways that we, as men, often do not feel comfortable admitting. I think we also tend to mistake longevity for resilience.

The more insular our world view becomes, the more liable we are to succumb to bitterness and resentment. The future looms like an imposing shadow, while the world we grew up in and understand recedes to the fringes. We are deprived of relevance and starved of the attention and privilege we once enjoyed. We are nostalgic for the imagined past. Do you see where I'm going with this?

Just as Andrew Tate preys on the insecurity of teenage boys, other bad actors stoke the flames of estrangement among older Australian men.

It's nothing new. Media empires have been built around it. But as I discussed earlier, the proliferation of the internet and the blossoming of innumerable new media outlets have diversified and muddied the already murky waters of truth and disinformation.

It's true that older Australians are increasingly using social-media sites, especially Facebook, as their primary source of news. It's also true that Facebook has faced serious criticism over its content moderation. *Breitbart* and the *Daily Wire*, two websites that shamelessly regurgitate debunked alt-right conspiracies, have consistently sat at the top of Facebook's engagement polls. Just as Andrew Tate has a direct line to thousands of Australian kids, these unscrupulous peddlers of shit have countless older people on the hook.

In the current media landscape, impotent rage is a hot commodity.

~

I'll end here on a personal note that I think illustrates what I've been talking about – our shared vulnerabilities.

I recently moved to Melbourne to be with my girlfriend. It wasn't the first time I've packed up my stuff and hit the road, so I thought I would be ready for the unsettling experience of having to build new connections in a new place, find employment and establish something of a comfortable equilibrium.

Let me tell you, friends: it was tough. The things that I thought would be forthcoming – fortune, a rich social life, a release from my vaping addiction – were not, and my regular support network was on the other side of this vast continent.

When our house was being painted, I found myself feverishly wandering around the streets of inner-north Melbourne. There was nothing to do at home except huff paint fumes, nothing to do outside but feel sorry for myself (and huff petrol fumes), while waiting for the good news to start miraculously rolling in.

I can now see that this period was terrible for my sense of self-worth, even though it did wonders for my step count. It also unveiled a streak of mean-spiritedness and insecurity that projected occasionally in nasty behaviour. I increasingly found myself becoming uncommunicative, ungrateful and generally a bit of a shit.

It took an argument over crockery and a small breakdown in front of my very patient girlfriend to realise that it probably wasn't about the crockery, and that I was experiencing the very things that I've been talking about in this chapter: the absence of community, isolation and, dare I say it, male loneliness. While I hope that, by the time of publication, I will have enjoyed immense wealth and social fulfilment, and I'm down to a few puffs at the pub, I think the move was an important reminder that even at the best of times, we are all only a few bad days or weeks away from cracking the shits and shutting ourselves off from the world.

My final bit of advice to Australian men, young and old, is this: touch grass, eat your two and five and be suspicious of anyone who tells you that you're hard done by.

I'm going to hand you back to Dad now. The next chapter, I think, is about him feeling sorry for himself.

Chapter 23

A Grumpy Relapse

Feeling sorry for myself? Yes, Hugh, I am, or at least I was earlier today.

Off to the gym this morning, I pulled over to allow a vehicle coming the other way to pass me on our narrow street. I waited; I wanted something in return. And I waited. And what I wanted didn't arrive.

There was no raised forefinger of acknowledgement. Of thanks. Nothing.

Bloody hell. Some people!

I've also just received a notification on my phone from Telstra, informing me that I have now earnt 10,000 rewards points. I am urged to go to the website to see how my loyalty will be rewarded. I click on. The website reveals that I am now only 22,700 points away from receiving a hair straightener. And as I scroll the prize page, I am literally ten lifetimes away from winning an iPad. I can only conclude I am not a winner at all. The email was generated by an algorithm that loves to fuck people over by promising them things they will never receive. As reward for their loyalty.

At the gym, I watch an enormous man in spandex attempting an extraordinary weightlifting feat. It requires his fearsome muscles to bulge, his temple to twitch, his balance to nearly topple and a squeal of rancid gas to explode from between his clenched buttocks. The weight drops to the earth. He is neither shocked or appalled or ashamed by his bodily emission.

And as I walk on my treadmill, going nowhere slowly but hoping to burn off a few chardonnay calories, I look up at a TV, where Benjamin Netanyahu is holding a press conference to justify the deaths of women and children in Rafah; he's followed by an Israel Defense Forces media robot in a starched olive uniform declaring that those kids were sadly collateral damage in a much bigger battle.

And I think to myself, today I am fucking cross.

Because we have apparently learnt nothing from the brutal misery of history. And today I am being stung by that truth. And here in the affluent, tut-tutting, always-judging West, governments have consciously decided not to respond or to save the lives of the innocent. What hypocritical bullshit artists we all are.

And a man who just farted with great freedom of self-expression did not say 'excuse me'.

I am so fed up, I abandon my exercise and go straight to Abhi's bakery, where I will seek solace in a chorizo and potato quiche. But when I get there, I realise they have closed early, because it is Saturday.

The silly and unimportant, the trivial and the deeply concerning, have all arrived across my consciousness within a few hours today. And I am, for now, drawn to its irresistible gloom. I am choosing to remain unreconciled, and quite furious at how unfair this world is – not to spoilt, privileged me, but to everyone who just hangs by a thread.

And I am sullen and frowning and grumpy. And having spent months

A Grumpy Relapse

at this keyboard urging you to not take it all so seriously, to not collect petty grievances as proof that everyone and everything is stupid, I pause.

And decide to go for a walk.

A woman with a French bulldog smiles at me. Grudgingly, I smile back.

Well, that's a start.

Chapter 24

A Visit to the Doctor

You probably think I covered this already. And I did. Remember those strong words of encouragement to go and see your GP, to tell them the truth and do as they say? To not kid yourself?

Well, I'm writing this to admit how easy and frankly convenient it is to forget or ignore good advice sometimes. Like on that grumpy Saturday I just told you about.

So the doctor beckons. I know what I should be doing; I just don't want to do it. I've even paused for a moment to fold my arms in a defiant and defensive gesture. Like a sulky five-year-old, or a sixty-five-year-old letter writer to the local newspaper, or Old Coot, or Lycra Larry. Or Dad.

Thing is, I dutifully had my bloods done a week or so ago, and today I'm off to my GP for the annual check-up. I should feel virtuous and sensible, because I know it is the right thing to do, but I feel strangely anxious.

I have been eating and drinking merrily since my last consultation – which, my friends, can happen with all this spare time available to us in retirement – and even though I'm getting plenty of exercise, what if my doctor looks at me disapprovingly? What if he feels today is the day to deliver a few home truths about my lifestyle choices? What if my blood tests reveal … something's wrong? You know, like really wrong. And weird.

What if I am one of only a handful of people on earth to be afflicted by Foreign Accent Syndrome or Walking Corpse Syndrome or Exploding Head Syndrome? They're real. I've googled them.

I am genuinely considering these scenarios while I have my shower and get dressed.

I haven't had any breakfast either. I'm starving. My wife suggests, with the patience of a mother speaking to that sulky five-year-old, that eating two slices of toast and Vegemite probably won't make much difference should I have to jump on the scales. I suck my gut in.

I know in my heart that it is time to remember and act on the advice I so breezily offered to you. So I read again what I have written. And I promise again not to lie to my doctor. I promise to understand that this is for my own good.

And yet I still put on a pair of lightweight shoes, just in case I'm weighed with footwear attached. I am veering towards the irrational. There is no reason to think this way. But I tell myself I can't help it.

I can. Don't be a dick.

~

When I do walk into the surgery, I calm down. The hard bit is getting here. I am doing the right thing.

Tick.

There is one patient ahead of me. I listen to his conversation with the receptionist. He is a fifty-four-year-old heavy-haulage driver and he has come for his annual medical. He is wearing shorts and a polo shirt and work boots. He rests both hands on the counter and appears to breathe with some effort. He's conspicuously overweight. This bloke is younger than me, but the nature of his work suggests his is a sedentary life. King of the Road, sitting high in his cab and knowing exactly which roadhouse serves the best crumbed cheese kransky. And within arm's reach at all times he'll have a stash of chocolate bars to keep the boredom at bay and his sugar levels up.

He looks weary. But at least he is here.

I hope he gets the certificate he needs to keep doing the job he no doubt loves and which presumably a family relies upon. But I wonder too how he'll look and feel this time next year. And when he gets to sixty.

I am reminded that these are his years, and my years, to make good decisions. Any lifestyle improvements we choose to value and prioritise today will benefit us as we get older.

And let's not kid ourselves, we all know that to be true.

So now it's my turn.

I know the surgery is short-staffed today – doctors off crook and some nursing staff have been lured away to work in aged care because, finally, there's a bit more money in it. Appointments will be brisk. That's fine with me. I make bright and breezy conversation with my attentive GP and then realise I am doing so partly to chew up the minutes. It's a bit pathetic.

The good doctor squints at his screen and tells me my bloods have come back looking good. He doesn't add 'for a man your age', so in my head I vainly inflate this to Trumpian conclusions, 'one of the best, maybe the best, who knows'.

I do offer a small self-aware admission about what I've been eating and drinking, but he waves away my concern with a mumbled observation that vaguely references 'portion control' or something that I don't quite catch. Because I don't really want to. Anyway, I nod enthusiastically. Into the home stretch and buoyed that my earlier fears are unwarranted.

As he takes my blood pressure, we chat amiably about GPs and their ongoing and fractious relationship with government – until he stops mid-sentence and points to the screen.

'Have a look at those numbers.'

I don't look at the numbers; I just stare into his eyes, trying to read if there is panic and dismay. There isn't.

My blood pressure is high. We agree many patients suffer from white-coat anxiety, which pushes their levels higher the moment they enter a surgery, and while I hope this too can be explained as a 'situational reading', he wants to be sure. He recommends I book myself in to wear a BP monitor for twenty-four hours to get a real sense of where it's at.

I will. I won't. I will. I haven't yet.

He then asks if I snore. I do. I can tell we are going to have a conversation about sleep apnoea at some point. I wonder if I should tell my wife that bit. We move on ...

I am not showing any sign of prostate cancer. And he describes the condition of my kidneys and liver as 'pristine'. I ask him if I can quote that to my wife. He nods. ('It's pristine, darl, an absolutely pristine liver. One of the best, maybe the best, who knows.')

And then our time is up. He hasn't even asked me to jump on the scales. As I gather my things, he smiles. 'You look well, Geoff.'

I carry those words out the door with me. Suddenly feeling lighter, happier and very sensible. Until, of course, I have to book in to wear that blood-pressure monitor so we can learn more about the capacity of my arteries to carry the burden of being me. I'm fascinated how quickly I begin to consider how I might skew the results. Perhaps if I spend twenty-four hours lying perfectly still?

~

I've included this feeble confession and the little chapter about my grumpy relapse to remind you, and me, that we remain works in progress. Whether we're forty-five or sixty-three or eighty-seven or about to die tomorrow. Works in progress.

Many of us do have some time and space, some opportunity and capacity to choose to attend to the niggles and doubts of life that make us grumpy and unwell. We won't resolve them all. Some will nag away. But if we make the effort to give ourselves the best chance of enjoying and appreciating the good things – some of which haven't even arrived yet – then doesn't it represent great opportunity? Something to work towards and look forward to.

Until something else pops up.

Like a diagnosis of Foreign Accent Syndrome or Walking Corpse Syndrome or Exploding Head Syndrome.

And then, I imagine, we'll deal with that too. In our own uniquely individual way.

Chapter 25

Finding Contentment

'Love This Life' by Crowded House is a favourite song of mine. Written by Neil Finn, it offers comfort to me the way religious verse might do for others (like Bruce Robinson). I reach for its words whenever something tears at the fragility of things. Love this life; it may be all we have.

Out walking the dog this morning, I came upon an old chap in a blue beanie trying to coax an equally arthritic little terrier to keep up. Or just keep going. The dog stopped for a wee and a sniff and managed to cadge a couple of cold chips dropped outside the pub last night.

'G'day,' I said, to both.

The man raised bushy eyebrows in acknowledgement.

'How are you?' I added. Uninvited and probably unnecessarily.

'Aagh,' he said, 'don't ask.'

And with a sorrowful smile, he lowered his head, and the pair went on their way.

A few minutes later, I was passed by a young man in a black hoodie with the words 'How to Make Meth' written in bold white type across his chest. I turned around to watch him walking. 'Instructions ...' covered his back in a smaller print I couldn't quite read. The kid had a swagger on. He wanted to be noticed. He wanted people like me to take a second look – and I'm guessing he was tuned in to hear annoyance or discomfort or even someone's quickening stride as they moved away.

Two momentary interactions with strangers introduced me to two very different men at very different stages of their lives. The young man wanting to make a statement of some kind, to assert himself. The old fella perhaps quietly trying to make sense of something that had gone wrong or been lost to him. 'Don't ask,' he'd said. He probably just wanted me to leave him alone.

Did I need reminding there are no one-size-fits-all versions of us? Perhaps I did. Perhaps we all do sometimes.

There is the universality of us and the specificity of you. Whatever suggestions I've offered so far, the conclusions I've drawn or the dodgy generalisations I have indulged – however much I try to cajole or annoy, in the hope of cheering you up or helping you go easy on yourself and those around you – we do all see the world from the life experience we carry in our heads. The accumulated moments that shape us and make us uniquely us.

In the pursuit of what? Survival? Happiness? What is happiness anyway?

Every year, a group of clever researchers and analysts come together to produce the World Happiness Report. A study of who the happiest humans are and where you'll supposedly find them. We may be unique, but we can always be measured collectively.

Something called the Cantril Ladder is used to determine levels of happiness by asking people to evaluate how good their life is on a scale of one to ten across six categories – GDP, how generous the general population is, how much welfare support exists, what your life expectancy is like and how free you feel to make your own life choices. Oh, and whether your country is corrupt or not. Top-rung happiness scores a ten; greatest unhappiness scores a zero.

And pretty much every year, the judges determine that our friends in Finland have got happiness pegged. In 2024, Finnish people – with an overall score of 7.741 – were again considered the happiest people on Earth. The other Nordic countries came in next. Australians, having climbed 7.057 rungs, were perched quite cheerfully at number ten in the World Happiness rankings.

In light of these findings, and given that Disneyland is sold to us as the happiest place on Earth, I've been trying to imagine what it's like when a horde of Heikkinens from Helsinki turn up to shake Mickey by the hand. Is it as blissful as it sounds? As happy as a human can be?

And what does that feel like?

Well...

A Finnish academic by the name of Professor Jukka Savolainen was interviewed by the BBC to explain the greater levels of happiness enjoyed in Northern European countries – and he put it down to a single Swedish word, *lagom*. It translates to something of which Goldilocks would wholeheartedly approve: 'Not too much, not too little, just right.'

Professor Savolainen went on to explain that Finns and Swedes and Danes don't mind living in modest homes and, unlike other peoples, have very little interest in the three-car garage. They like public transport – apparently, because it arrives and leaves regularly and on time. They like nature, because it exists right outside their window and hasn't yet been bulldozed. They broadly have faith in politicians and government and bureaucracies. And things seem to work.

The Finns appear to be a high-trust people. They expect a better 'us' and they believe they get it.

Now, I'm not here to promote Finland as proof of a socialist utopia – the weather is awful, the language is utterly baffling and I'm told the people enjoy long silences that can discomfort strangers – but there is something to be said for humans who appreciate the idea of 'balance' and 'enough' and who, if they can help it, would prefer not to leave big greasy fingerprints all over the Earth. They seem ...

Well, here's the word I prefer.

Content.

~

And on that ...

For many years, I hosted an interview series on the wireless called *Who Are You?*. Conventional in many ways, it was an intimate exploration of the lives of some quite interesting people, and each episode ended with me asking that same question I asked my dad: 'Are you happy?'

Over time, and watching my guests often struggle with the presumptuous expectation associated with the question, I decided to change it. I asked them something more reflective.

'Are you content?'

It seemed a much truer measure of a life. And from their responses, the conclusion I drew was that to be content is to have ... got this far. Done one's best. Appreciated the good times and battled through the bad. Accepted one's mistakes but not been a prisoner of regret.

Everyone I asked preferred the idea of contentment to the fleeting and episodic nature of happiness, because it seemed to acknowledge a more realistic aspiration.

And I guess contentment comes with a degree of awareness and acceptance.

This is where we are. And we have a finite amount of time left. So how do we want to spend it?

When we genuinely stop to consider it, the question becomes profound, doesn't it? How do we wish to spend the rest of our lives? What will we prioritise? What will matter most?

It's really strange to me that we don't invest in these questions the way we do other landmark decisions in our lives. I guess we hope for the best. Just like retirement.

Well, imagine what we could do if we put some real thought into it. Committed to a plan. Created goals and strategies for how they might be reached.

Rather than trawling over professional and personal failures, or picking at the scabs of our mistakes, what if we decide to actively pursue and shape the next stage of our life as positively as we can?

A form of contentment insurance.

When I think of that Neil Finn lyric about loving *this* life, I am reminding myself to bank the good days. Because, on another day, I might need the warm reassurance of that memory. And I don't know when that day will arrive, but it will.

We're nearer to the end than the start.

~

The end of this little handbook, anyway.

How long did it take us to get here?

Me? A couple of years.

You? Maybe you've read it in one feverish night and your life has already changed for the better.

That's brilliant.

Maybe you've dipped in and out of it and at least it's got you thinking about the bloke you are or want to be.

Terrific.

Maybe you managed a couple of pages and, using the language of Elon Musk, declared it part of the woke mind virus and went outside to mow the lawn.

Although the Victa wouldn't start.

You don't have to consider any of this if you don't want to. You can tell the whole concept of this book, and me specifically, to fuck off. But ...

If we stop caring and stop engaging, our world will just shrink, and we will become increasingly agitated and impatient and cynical. And no fun to be around at all.

Remember that line from AC Grayling? It's about hanging our beliefs and prejudices out on the clothesline, like bedsheets, and letting them flap about in a fresh breeze, before we bring them in and decide if they are still relevant and valid and important. Or whether they are not – and perhaps then we can just let them go.

Imagine the relief of letting go of old grievances. And all that negativity. And all that cynicism.

~

Now there's a word I have come to reassess over time.

When I was barely twenty years old, I was working as a sports reporter at *Nine News* in Perth. Our chief of staff was one of the most hilarious, black-humoured individuals I had come across in my young life. He could eviscerate with his words. A hilarious bully.

One day he said to me, 'You are the most cynical twenty-year-old I have ever met.'

I took that as high praise. Being called cynical at a tender age told me I already had a handle on the world and all its bullshit and insincerity. I felt razor-sharp and perfectly equipped for journalism.

But as the years went by, I began to see cynicism in a very different light.

Cynicism doesn't have faith or believe in anything. It casts never-ending doubt. It punctures the possibility of a new idea ever working, so why would you bother trying? It sneers at people. And I have come to conclude that the wandering minstrel Billy Bragg is right: cynicism is the enemy of hope.

Even if you are correct and get to point to the scoreboard and say, 'See, I was right all along,' you've still killed hope. You've caused someone else to doubt the value in believing in the possibility of something.

And the clincher for me? It stops being funny.

~

As I have wondered about your life, and yes, presumed much about it, I have also had to consider mine. And sitting for what must be thousands of hours at this desk – admittedly eating lunch, drinking beer, trawling social media and watching videos of dwarves wrestling when I should have been writing – I've begun to reappraise who I am and how I present to the world.

And I have committed to exploring what comes next.

The fact is, writing this book has been good for me too. I couldn't ask you all those questions without wanting to answer some myself.

I am more aware now, I hope, about how I speak to people and the interest I take in their conversation and their stories. More aware how I sound to others and of whether I am a generous listener and an empathetic friend. Those audits that were once part of my professional career are now even more important to me privately.

I am learning too not to presume anything about this new life I lead. Or succumb to that cynicism to which I was once drawn.

And I don't want to take anything for granted.

Tonight, I spoke to my best man. He was that, thirty-two years ago, and he still is.

A few months ago, he lost his adored older brother, who died suddenly in Sydney, collapsing while out jogging. My friend lives in London now, and while in the days that followed his terrible news, I expressed my great concern and sorrow, I didn't really think to follow up. I did not think to contact him a month on and say, 'How are you feeling, mate? And how can I help?'

I probably had a bit on at home and just assumed he'd push on. I sort of forgot. Such a bloke's reaction.

Tonight, on a whim, induced by a Sicilian red and a sudden swirling affection, I needed to call him. And after the requisite banter, he began to reveal how he was dealing with his grief and the accompanying brooding contemplation of his own mortality. He also told me of his plans to fly home to Australia and comfort his sister-in-law and the kids and just about everyone who knew his brother – none of whom knew him as well as he did.

Tonight, I promised him I would get on a plane and come and see him. To be there and to give him a hug.

Admittedly, he will have to keep finding me amusing even in his darkest hour, but he's sent me a message promising to 'practise my spontaneous laugh'.

And as I sit here, I know I should have reacted more quickly.

This is what we need to do for our mates. To be there and to be accountable. To love them as they love us and not be afraid to frame that as a fundamental truth and a key to living a meaningful life.

~

What else have I learnt?

Well, yes, it's true that time may be running out, but strangely I now have a lot more of it available to me. Not enough to join the RAAF as a fighter pilot or make it through qualifying and beat Carlos Alcaraz in the Wimbledon final, but enough to make some life adjustments, try some new things and see if I can be useful to others.

And yet all this time can ensnare us if we're not careful. We can become bored and restless and a bit narky because there's nothing in the diary to look forward to beyond a sphincter-tightening doctor's appointment next Friday. And with so much time available to reflect and ponder, we may well draw negative conclusions about the world and our place in it.

It is – as my son, Hugh, wrote earlier – as seductive for the young as it is for the old: the conclusion that we don't matter.

That's the time to push back.

It's time to learn how to tap dance. Or play the euphonium. Or make any of Ottolenghi's bewildering recipes. Or call your best man. Or best mate. Or that bloke you remember you really liked, but who you didn't quite make the effort to get in touch with again.

Do it.

And start to hear yourself responding to life's invitations with a 'yes' rather than the reflex of 'no'.

And to get us through all this – the good and the bad of post-career lives and wonky hips and fading memory and the fact that one day we may spend our hours picking specks of light off the walls and putting them in invisible baskets – we are going to need the help and support of those who love us. And they are going to need us too.

Remember what I said about our partners?

(Cue one last blast of the air-raid siren.)

They may have wider ambitions than we do now. Their bucket list might be full to overflowing, while we might prefer to stay at home. Well, that's fine. But we had better not get all sulky and self-pitying when they give us a peck on the cheek and say, 'See you in six weeks!' Because we could have gone with them. If we packed the right attitude.

So find it, pack it and go on the adventure.

And if you do insist on staying home and being a grumpy bugger, because you actually quite like being a grumpy bugger, well at least make a comic virtue of it. Becoming a funny bugger is a whole lot more satisfying than being called a miserable one.

So do continue to make lists of things that really piss you off. Other people's stupid. Just remember to keep reading them aloud so you are accountable for them. Make sure you have the Pythons' Cheese Shop bouzouki music playing in your head as you shout your grievances into the bathroom mirror or the roaring winds blowing off a raging sea. And then have a laugh about them.

The sheer fucking absurdity of them.

And you.

And us.

Go on, I know you want to.

~

'Da, da, da, dum, da dum, da dum ...'

- The way your son-in-law keeps trying to explain Bitcoin to you and why you should pull some money out of your super to invest in it. Honestly, mate, fuck off, I don't care.
- Entire walls of supermarket space given over to flavoured dips. Smoked vomit with rose and pistachios. Pre-chewed, suck-through-a-straw indicators of what our nutritional nursing home futures will look like. Ooh, that bunion-and-smegma combo is gorgeous. I like it slathered on warm pide.
- Those Republicans who taped sanitary napkins to their ears in the days after the assassination attempt on Donald Trump in a show of their loyalty. Lend me your fucking morons.
- The lowlife who stole the small frangipani from the front garden last night.
- The kid up the street who rides an electric scooter but won't wear a helmet.

- The fact your wife continues to buy that Danish butter when we have perfectly good cows here.
- The article that just revealed you can buy face cream these days made from bull's semen.
- And how no one seems to be able to separate the truth from all the bull – forget the semen – shit anymore.
- And how no one cares.
- And all hope seems lost.

Okay, pull back.

Maybe only prepare a list when you feel strong and able enough to pull out individual moments of such nonsensical stupidity and roar with laughter rather than succumb to tears.

Love this life.

Chapter 26

Imagine It

For all the words I've written, all the scenarios I've tried to bring to life, there's a simple scene that's played out in my head right from the beginning. And I imagine you in it.

It's a celebratory function of some kind, and there are perhaps a hundred people there. Quite a crowd. It might be related to family or a gathering of work colleagues. There are cocktails aplenty.

I look around and see you on the fringes with a drink in your hand, chatting and smiling. Happy to occupy that space, rather than a tight circle of those who are deemed most important.

And when I look over again, someone is telling you a story. They are very animated and you appear engaged. You may not have met this person before tonight, and perhaps this conversation is without consequence, but it doesn't really matter these days. You're keen and curious.

It did matter once, of course. Who you spoke to and what was said. You were compelled, perhaps, to shake certain hands and laugh at the jokes of someone who wasn't funny, but who was the chief financial officer from Sydney. Maybe you *were* the CFO from Sydney, telling the jokes and looking out to see who laughed loudest.

So many hierarchies and pecking orders. Deals to be done, contracts to be won. Wins to be had, approval to be earnt. Tension in your shoulders and shallow breaths passing your dry lips.

Do you remember?

When blokes like you made all the decisions? When blokes like you took ownership and responsibility for most of what life could throw at you? When blokes like you were expected to be solid and stoic and reliable and just get things done?

Even if you were shit-scared and didn't have a clue. And were promoted anyway. Or sacked without consideration.

Well, tonight, none of that seems to matter as you stand back and take in the room – filled with the hum of chatter and affirmations about how delicious the mushroom arancini balls are. There is no game to win. Certainly no demand on you to appraise or evaluate or declare, 'If I may have your attention, please, ladies and gentlemen.' Someone else will do that.

You are just glad to be here, particularly now you have caught the eye of the waiter with the chilli prawn vol-au-vents. Your shirt collar is not chafing; you are no longer in uniform. You are comfortable in your skin.

And there is a lightness.

~

I know the scenario might sound pissingly naive.

A Geoff Hutchison Hallmark card.

Me looking at you standing in a soft light seemingly unburdened and completely at your ease.

Well, it's not pissingly naive, because yesterday I described it to an old friend who is the CEO of a big public entity. His job is pressure-filled and he's bloody good at it. Only occasionally does he creak under the weight of the workload. You can spot his physical and emotional fatigue a mile off. My friend is always under professional scrutiny. The high-profile networks in which he moves require his almost-endless attendance at work functions and cocktail parties and important dinners, after which he'll often go back to the office and work late into the evening, perusing an inbox that never empties.

When I explained my scenario to him, and how the central character seems to be so relaxed and untroubled in a crowd, a beatific smile drifted across my friend's face and he closed his eyes. It was as if I had just described our imminent arrival in nirvana or promised him a lifetime of bacon sandwiches without any of the cancer-inducing consequences. It was as if he was Lenny and I was George, and I was telling him about the rabbits – although fans of Steinbeck will be delighted to know I didn't then shoot him for his own good.

My friend breathed deeply, allowed his eyes to open and fix on me and declared emphatically, 'I wish that was me.'

Simple as that.

'I wish that was me.'

He said, 'Everyone thinks I'm so gregarious and extroverted because I go to these events all the time and shake everyone's hand and make speeches.' He paused for a moment before confessing, 'It's all an act.'

He looked away, wondering perhaps if he should have let such a truth leak. But then he turned back and owned it.

'It's all an act.'

~

This, I think, is why I've written this book.

Conclusion

Needing to Hear Dad's Voice

After Hugh hurt his eye and was being prepared for emergency surgery at the Royal Victorian Eye and Ear Hospital, I rang my parents. Mum, to whom I was close, answered the phone and bore the first telling of the story, yet it was Dad with whom I needed to speak.

I'm unable to explain it, even today. It was Dad's voice I needed to hear.

And when he took the receiver and I explained again what happened, I began to cry.

I can't really remember what he said to me, but I can recall the faint echoes of a signal being sent from a father to his son. My dad to me.

He'll be okay.

You'll be okay.

Steady, steady.

At eighty-one years of age, my dad, on the other side of the country and at the other end of a phone line, was still able to steer me to safety, long after I imagined such a thing was possible or that I might have need of it.

But I needed it.

And he did it with quiet words of reassurance and affirmation and love.

~

Are there still important roles for us to play in the lives of others?

Can we blokes, as we age, push past the battle-weary fatigue and frustration that makes us grumpy and sad and threatens to envelope us and harden our hearts to the world?

I think you know the answer.

You've come this far.

Resources

If you need to talk to someone about your mental health or wellbeing, you can contact the following services:

- **MensLine Australia** – Help, support, referrals and counselling services for men on 1300 78 99 78, mensline.org.au.
- **Australian Men's Shed Association** – A collection of independent, community-based Men's Sheds to represent, support and promote face-to-face sharing of information and experiences, mensshed.org.
- **FriendLine** – For anyone who's feeling lonely, needs to reconnect or just wants to chat, on 1800 424 287, friendline.org.au.
- **HealthDirect** – Information and links for men experiencing any type of mental-health issue, heatlhdirect.gov.au/mens-mental-health.
- **Beyond Blue** – Information and support for a range of mental-health issues on 1300 22 4636, beyondblue.org.au.
- **Lifeline** – A hotline for crisis support and suicide prevention available 24 hours Australia-wide on 13 11 14, lifeline.org.au.
- **Suicide Call Back Service** – Free phone and online counselling for

people affected by suicide on 1300 659 467, suicidecallbackservice.org.au.